To Chrissy —

Enjoy the memories
these pages bring of
happy days at
Garrison Forest School!

Sarah
Achenbach

A
CENTURY
of
1910   *2010*
SPIRIT

GARRISON FOREST SCHOOL

by Sarah Achenbach

DESIGNED BY WENDY TRIPP RUFFIN '86

OWINGS MILLS, MARYLAND

Published by Garrison Forest School, 300 Garrison Forest Road, Owings Mills, Maryland, 21117, United States of America. www.gfs.org

ISBN 978-0-615-33691-6

Library of Congress Control Number: 2009913098

A Century of Spirit: Garrison Forest School / Sarah Achenbach

Designed by Wendy Tripp Ruffin, Garrison Forest School Class of 1986.

A Century of Spirit: Garrison Forest School was designed using Adobe InDesign CS3.
The book was printed on McCoy Silk 100 lb. text using vegetable-based inks.
The typefaces in the book are Caslon 540, Trajan, and Helvetica Neue.
Printed in the United States of America by J.W. Boarman, Inc., Baltimore, Maryland on a Man Roland Press.

All images have been professionally reproduced to the best image quality possible.

Garrison Forest School is an independent, all-girls' day school, kindergarten through twelfth grade, with a regional, national, and international residential program beginning in eighth grade, and a coed preschool.

"I've so often tried—

only to find the words as elusive

as this 'grace' they try to describe—

all I can say is it

[the Garrison Forest spirit]

must have been part of this school

from the beginning.

And each generation has treasured it

and been proud of it,

as you are proud of a goodly heritage.

Maybe it gives you confidence,

maybe you walk a little higher

for knowing it's part of you,

maybe you're glad to share it,

maybe you take a special joy

in meeting a challenge.

It's like a little compass

that over the years in good times

and bad times,

today perhaps as never before,

has kept Garrison Forest on course.

Perhaps last and most of all,

it's a sense of belonging."

—Nancy Jenkins Offutt
Co-Headmistress, Garrison Forest School, 1929 - 1960

TABLE OF CONTENTS

FOREWORD

Reaching the century landmark is a milestone by any measure. But for an educational institution to celebrate its centennial with a program and purpose very much in the 21st century, yet deeply grounded in its founding mission, is remarkable.

A Century of Spirit: Garrison Forest School explores Garrison Forest School of 1910 and of 2010, and nearly every year in between. The facts and dates serve as markers for key moments in our school's history, but we have also taken great care to celebrate our community's character and characters. The perhaps indefinable, yet palpable, Garrison Forest spirit is as much a part of our school's history as any event, faculty member, or building. Nowhere is that spirit more evident than in the resiliency, authenticity, and humanity of our alumnae and students. There is something different about a Garrison girl—I believe this in my heart.

In fact, it is this spirit that I admire most about Garrison Forest School. It took courage and vision to found a girls' school in 1910 at a time when the country denied women the right to vote and college for women was still a radical idea. Think of the history this school went on to witness. Two world wars. The Great Depression. The Civil Rights Movement. The Women's Movement. The Information Age. Through each decade, through lean times and growth, Garrison Forest has had the remarkable ability to transform itself at key times, by intention or by providence.

The steel will, charm, and old-fashioned gumption of co-headmistresses Jean G. Marshall and Nancy J. Offutt enabled the school not just to survive the Great Depression, but thrive, by strengthening the boarding and academic programs. Decades later, during the financially grim 1970s when girls' schools were closing or merging with other schools, Garrison Forest once again proved its ability to adapt. In 1975, The Valley School merged with us to return our educational model to its founding version: all-girls, first through twelfth grade, with a residential program and a coeducational preschool.

The 21st-century Garrison Forest continues to embrace possibilities with leading-edge experiential learning programs for girls in science and engineering, public health, leadership, and public service. Our new endeavors are bold, purposeful responses to today's educational challenges, but in many ways they are business as usual for Garrison Forest School. For 100 years, this school has embraced the vision, courage, passion, and perseverance of its founders and leaders and pushed ahead. These pages bear witness to this remarkable achievement. It is an inspiring story, and we hope, a great read.

G. Peter O'Neill, Jr.
Head of Garrison Forest School

AUTHOR'S NOTE

I received a lot of advice and opinions during my three-year-plus adventure in writing *A Century of Spirit: Garrison Forest School*. Nearly all the advice was good, but I chose the wisdom of the March Hare, who told Alice simply to "start at the beginning, and when you get to the end, stop." In trying to capture Garrison Forest from 1910 to 2010, that is essentially what I have attempted to do.

I interviewed dozens of people in person, by phone, and through electronic mail. I scoured the shelves of the school's archives, pondered and puzzled, researched and re-researched, wrote and re-wrote. I have made every attempt to present a thorough, factual history that is informative and entertaining, but could not include every event and person that has been a vital part of Garrison Forest's history. The events included have been carefully corroborated by the archives' documented sources, and any errors are mine. Alumnae names are written as they appear in the GFS Class News; all other names are presented with titles.

A great deal of the school's history, though, was gleaned from personal recollection by alumnae, current and former faculty, administrators, staff, and friends of GFS. I discovered time and again that people often remember the same event completely differently. This is where the documented facts intersect and intertwine with the rich oral history of Garrison Forest to create something I found to be magical. The stories of this school have helped to shape successive generations of Garrison girls, and these stories are simply the best way to try to put the Garrison Forest spirit into words.

The larger story of Garrison Forest's founding as a small country school and its tenacious transformation into a thriving, internationally recognized leader in girls' education is told through the tenures of the school's heads. I have attempted to offer a glimpse into their personalities, mettle, and the flavor of the times in which they led. After following the March Hare's advice, I arrived at the end (at least for the first 100 years), and discovered what I had known all along: Garrison Forest's impressive history and indelible spirit were forged from the character of those who studied, taught, or worked here, lived or laughed here. My hope is that the personality of the school—its warmth and welcoming sense of community— shines through each page. I dedicate this book to all the Garrison Forest alumnae who have shared their memories with me.

Sarah Achenbach

Class time in the early years.

MARY MONCRIEFFE LIVINGSTON
FOUNDING HEADMISTRESS, 1910-1929

On a cloudy morning in late September 1910, a handful of children left their homes, boarded a train, and rode it to the end of the Northern Central Railway's Green Spring Valley Branch line. Others hopped on the electric streetcar on the Emory Grove line and rattled and swayed along the streetcar tracks that lined the east side of Reisterstown Turnpike. A few hitched a pony to a cart and bumped along beside mule-drawn farm wagons, horse and buggies, and a smattering of automobiles. Still other children walked alongside the Turnpike's dusty, dirt-and-stone-packed two lanes, the girls' hair bows and boys' sailor-suit kerchiefs bobbing. The final leg of the journey for the nearly two dozen children was the climb up a wide, tree-lined driveway to the house at the top of the hill.

It was the first day of school.

The schoolhouse, with its white clapboards and a large, welcoming porch, was a stately country manor with views of the rolling Green Spring Valley. The house and grounds (and its one cow and several chickens) must have been an imposing sight to the nervous schoolchildren that cloudy morning. But waiting for them was a woman whose warmth, graciousness, and grace would set the tone that first day—and for thousands of school days over the next century.

During the summer of 1910, Mary Moncrieffe Livingston, a 41-year-old schoolteacher from Kingston, New York, rented a farmhouse and stable to open a school in rural Baltimore County. The formal name of the school was the Green Spring Valley School, though people referred to it as "Miss Livingston's School," or more commonly "Garrison Forest School" because of its proximity to the Garrison Forest region of the valley. The school's nickname became the official name in 1938 when the school incorporated.

Miss Livingston was no stranger to the Green Spring Valley or to the business of running a school. In 1903, she had founded and served as principal for the Livingston School for Children in Kingston, New York, for boys and girls ages four to 14. Her home doubled as schoolhouse and residence for a handful of female boarders, an arrangement she would replicate in Maryland.

Mary Moncrieffe Livingston.

An advertisement for Miss Livingston's school in Kingston, New York.

An early advertisement for Garrison Forest School in the *Redbook Magazine*. At its founding, the school enrolled girls from the nursery program through the twelfth grade. From 1910-48, boys attended GFS through the primary grades, though most left to attend boys' schools after second grade. By 1948, the school was solely all-girls and offered fifth through twelfth grade only. Boys in the early grades returned as GFS students after the 1975 merger with The Valley School, a nearby preschool and elementary school.

An early mode of transportation to school.

Long before Garrison Forest School opened its doors, Miss Livingston's petite frame, kind blue eyes, and up-swept blonde hair were familiar sights to many families. In 1889, her sister Esther Livingston married the Reverend Dr. Hobart Smith, Rector of St. Thomas' Church, an Episcopal church on Garrison Forest Road. Miss Livingston and her family—mother Esther Dibblee Livingston (widow of Moncrieffe Livingston) and brother Robert—were frequent visitors to the St. Thomas' Rectory.[1]

As the 1909 Christmas season approached, Miss Livingston and her mother prepared for their holiday visit to St. Thomas'. Meanwhile, the Green Spring Valley was abuzz with talk about the need for a new school. Local educational options were few and quite literally far between, and a buggy ride to one of the private schools in Baltimore City was arduous and long. By the turn of the century, many of the area's small public schools had all but disappeared. Though Garrison or Tobinsville School, one of the first public schools in the area, had been operating since 1849, its one room held only grades one through six. St. Thomas', too, had operated a small school off and on since the mid-1800s, and several families in the area sent their children there, while others employed private tutors. Families in the St. Thomas' congregation and across the valley knew of Miss Livingston's experience and were anxious to talk with her.

During the Christmas holiday, Mrs. Smith hosted a tea so that ladies in the community interested in possibly opening a new school could meet Miss Livingston. The women in attendance assured the guest of honor that she would lack neither resources nor students should she choose to establish a neighborhood school.[2] Miss Livingston politely declined. In the following months, though, she found that her sister's chronic poor health meant she and her mother would need to relocate to the Greenspring Valley, and so she had a change of heart about establishing a school.[3] She set about finding a house to rent to serve as both school and home to her and her mother, and by September 25, 1910, Miss Livingston welcomed her first pupils to Garrison Forest School.[4]

From the beginning, GFS accepted both day and boarding students. The earliest known advertisement for the school notes that "The Garrison Forest School…[gives] the combined advantage of a real home in the country and a thoroughly good school; boarding department for girls from 6 to 16 years…pupils may also be entered as five-day boarders." Miss Livingston set tuition that first year at $100 and produced a small play with students, a fairy tale, designed to "whet the interest" of local families. She also hired a handful of women teachers to instruct primary and intermediate classes in art, arithmetic, English, French, Latin, and music.

Though it may have been family circumstances that drew Miss Livingston to Maryland, she threw herself into running her new school. However, she herself did not teach. Her talent was in administration. With a kind nature, ready sympathy, and gentle spirit, she ably led students and faculty, beginning every school day with hymns and prayers. Students were expected to curtsey "Good Morning" to her. Hers was a personality that students—and their children—long remembered. From the earliest yearbook on record (1920) until 1929, the year Miss Livingston retired, yearbook dedications spoke of her courage, conviction, and uncompromising principles.

George Wills, the son of Margaret Marees Wills '24, fondly remembered numerous boyhood visits to Miss Livingston in the late 1940s. By then, Miss Livingston was retired and renting a room at the Ten Mile House in Reisterstown. "My mother and I would have tea with Miss Livingston," he recalled. "I would have to wear a jacket or my McDonogh uniform, and my mother would always remind me not to speak to Miss Livingston until she spoke to me. She would shake my hand and put her other hand on top of it, and ask, 'How are you, George?' " He considered Miss Livingston a second grandmother, calling her an icon: "There was an elegance about her, but not in an austere or ostentatious way. I remember the warmth of her smile and her affection." Edith Ney, one of two students in the first graduating class in 1914 and a former faculty member, remarked, "Much that we learned to treasure never came from books but from the gracious and generous personality who presided over our goings out and comings in."

BURSTING AT THE SEAMS

By 1912, Miss Livingston's rented schoolhouse was bursting at the seams with day students and a handful of boarders. On March 12 of that year, a group of seven business-minded fathers, led by Laurence M. Miller and John McHenry, met at the Green Spring Valley Hunt Club to form a corporation to support the burgeoning school. The directors of the newly created Green Spring Valley School, Inc., offered $10,000 in capital stock, with 180 shares totaling $9,000 held by the gentlemen who served as founding directors. Miss Livingston set an asking price of $1,000 for her school, for which she was paid 20 shares of common stock.

At the corporation's first business meeting, held the next day at Miss Livingston's home, the directors presided over an agenda that would set

The original home of Garrison Forest School from 1910 to 1912, the property at 1725 Reisterstown Road served as both schoolhouse and home to Miss Livingston. Classrooms were on both the first and second floors, and those students who arrived by pony cart would board their horses in the stables behind the house. In the late 1920s, Dr. Palmer F. Williams purchased the house as his office and home, seeing patients from across the region, (Miss Livingston, Miss Marshall, and Miss Offutt among them), and serving as the school doctor to Garrison Forest from 1930 to 1974, as well as Gilman School, Dr. Williams' alma mater. When I-695 (the Baltimore Beltway) was completed in 1962, the house was razed to accommodate the Pikesville/Reisterstown Road interchange.

Laurence M. Miller (1874-1950), pictured in his Episcopal High School baseball uniform, was Garrison Forest's founding President of the Board of Trustees. A resident of Pikesville and a well-respected insurance executive with the Northwestern Mutual Life Insurance Company, Mr. Miller, along with John McHenry, led a group of men in gathering interest for the fledgling school and for financing the school's move to its present site in 1912. The school's founding fathers (Mr. Miller, Mr. McHenry, Arthur H. Hall, Charles M. Stewart, Jr., Redmond C. Stewart, Frederick C. Todd, and John Sawyer Wilson, Jr.) each had children enrolled in Garrison Forest in 1910. The Stewart and McHenry families would have successive generations of sons and daughters attend Garrison Forest.

Capital stock for The Green Spring Valley School, Inc., totaled $10,000, while common stock was offered at $50 per share. Interestingly, Dr. Williams witnessed Miss Livingston's stock certificate.

the school's course for the next century. They unanimously voted to accept Miss Livingston's offer, making her a stockholder and entitling her to one vote. The board elected officers, choosing Mr. Miller, the majority stockholder with 10 shares, as president and John McHenry as vice president. The meeting's crucial agenda item, though, was the business of finding a suitable property as the permanent home for Garrison Forest School. Mr. Stewart, a GFS father and an attorney with Semmes, Bowen & Semmes in Baltimore, reported that he had signed a contract on behalf of the corporation to purchase a farm owned by Mrs. Adam Deupert, located less than three miles up Reisterstown Turnpike from the current schoolhouse. For the $23,500 purchase price, Garrison Forest School received 10 acres, a garage/stable, one horse, one cow, a Dayton buggy, a few farming implements, and a stately house known as Manor House set at the top of a winding lane.

Over the next few months, Miss Livingston and the school community prepared for the move. The first-ever school admissions catalogues were printed, Mrs. John McHenry was named president of a new, 17-member Ladies' Advisory Board, and Miss Livingston and her mother moved into Manor House. The Northern Central Railroad even added a new train to its daily schedule, with one leaving Baltimore's Calvert Street Station at 8:10 a.m. to carry children to Garrison station.

On October 2, 1912, Miss Livingston began her first year in the new location with 30 students (including three boarders) and an important new staff member: Mrs. Roscoe Ney, mother of boarder Edith and a friend of Miss Livingston's from Kingston. In exchange for room and board, Mrs. Ney was the first GFS housemother. By the end of the 1912-13 school year, the corporation netted a profit of $694. Miss Livingston's salary remained as it had been from the founding year: room and board plus $50 per month during the school year and $25 a month during the summer months. She lived in one of the large rooms on the second floor of Manor House with views of the front lawn. Kay Dorr Sommers '33 wrote that "students entered [Miss Livingston's room] only on the occasion of reprimand for some particularly heinous misdeed."

Students in 1912.

SCHOOL DAYS

Life at Garrison Forest followed the expected rituals of school. Each morning all students and teachers assembled in the front hall of Manor House for hymns and prayers, and then proceeded to their classrooms, the primary grades bustling up the stairs to their second-floor classrooms (bedrooms were used as classrooms) and the older students remaining on the first floor. Kay Sommers fondly recalled the post-lunch free hour which she and other "Moncrieffe dwellers often spent in a running game of Blackjack." Afternoon activities included outdoor basketball, riding, tennis, and swimming at the YMCA in Baltimore.

As a simple country school, Garrison Forest nonetheless designed its earliest curriculum to prepare young women for college. The only two members of the first graduating class in 1914, Edith Ney and Constance Irvin, passed the rigorous college entrance exam for Bryn Mawr College. A non-college-preparatory program also was offered, with each graduate receiving a certificate instead of a diploma. This practice continued at GFS through the 1940s. Miss Livingston stressed first, though, above any academic achievement or program, strength of character and high moral ideals, qualities implied in her chosen motto for the school: *Esse Quam Videri*—To Be Rather Than to Seem.

The school also moved to the rhythms of country life. Once, when a cow was going to have a calf, French teacher Mademoiselle Gilles excused all her classes for the day so that she and her students could spend the

A dormitory room in Moncrieffe in the 1920s.

Students studying in the library in Moncrieffe.

15

"It was just after the turn of the century and as there was not a sufficient supply of young ladies, the school was forced to give us boys a break to get a starting quota for the school. We had moved from Dr. Williams' house to the present site and used to expend excess energy playing touch football in which the young ladies insisted in joining us. Miss Livingston frowned on this, being sure some of her girls were going to be hurt and in this she was partly right. We rapidly progressed from touching to tackling, as that more definitely fixed the position of the ball. Then it happened — one of the skinny, tough ladies was scampering along with the pigskin and ran right over our right tackle, knocking several fingers out of joint. This necessitated first aid and Miss Livingston went from frowning to positive action and football of any sort was banned. I think the only lesson we learned was that the female of the species is more deadly than the male!"

— Nevett Steele, GFS alumnus and one of the original students in 1910.

whole day in the stable. Each day, horses and ponies—still a common mode of transportation to and from school—were tied to the hitching post next to Manor House or boarded in the stable. Classes were held rain or shine, snow or ice. The only uniforms were for Upper School athletics. Beyond that, students simply wore what they had to class.

Lois Bryan Wood '20, one of the original students in 1910, recalled that "everything depended on the streetcar as to when school opened or closed. We all raced up the path and tore our hats and coats off. Mademoiselle Gilles would sound the chord and then we marched in… at 1:30 [we] all tore down to the streetcar to get the one that ran back at 1:40 to town." For the boarding students, weekend activities consisted of Saturday morning sock-darning sessions in Manor House and compulsory church attendance at St. Thomas' every Sunday morning. Sunday afternoons featured heavily chaperoned teas at the school with "Romeos," the girls' nicknames for the suitors who would come calling.

WEEK DAY SCHEDULE	
Rising Bell	7 A. M.
Breakfast	7.45 A. M.
Breakfast, Sundays	9 A. M.
Outdoor exercise	8.30 A. M.—8.50 A. M.
Opening of School	8.50 A. M.—9.00 A. M.
Recitations	9.00 A. M.—11.35 A..M
Recess	11.35 A. M.—11.50 A. M.
Recitations	11.50 A. M.—1.50 P. M.
Lunch	2.00 P. M.—2.30 P. M.
Rest hour and dressing time for Sports and Riding	2.30 P. M.—3.00 P. M.
	4.15 P. M.

GARRISON FOREST AND WORLD WAR I

By April 1917, when the United States joined World War I, Garrison Forest was entering into its own era of change. In June 1916, the corporation posted its first deficit of $346. The following year, with the war on, tuition accounts fell off by approximately $1,500, and nearly $2,000 was outstanding in tuition payments. To help meet its operating budget, trustees voted to increase tuition by 20 percent, the first tuition increase since the school's founding.

The Great War also required the school to close for a few days during the fall harvest season. With many farmers and field hands off fighting overseas, help was needed in nearby cornfields, so GFS students picked corn instead of going to classes. The so-called Farmerettes donated their wages to the war relief. The home front also proved a source of entertainment of sorts for the older Garrison Forest girls. Lois Wood recalled the many U.S. Army trucks that passed by the school on the now-paved Reisterstown Road: "We were just old enough to have eyes for the young men. We would waste all the time in the world waving to the Army trucks."

Prior to the war, Mr. Miller made, perhaps, his most transformative decision as president: In 1915, he invited George M. Shriver, friend and fellow GFS parent, to join him as a trustee. As an executive with the Baltimore & Ohio Railroad, Mr. Shriver was a natural choice to help guide the school on the right financial track. On June 4, 1918, Mr. Miller resigned from the GFS board to serve in the U.S. Army. Mr. Shriver was elected president, a position he would hold until his death in 1942. His quiet, steady leadership and largesse would see the school through financial hardship and social change.

Ice skating on a nearby pond was a popular activity in the 1920s. In 1937 it became a school sport.

Handling lawn chores with a horse-drawn rotary mower.

Students in the 1910s and 1920s did not wear a school uniform.

"Reddy," an Auburn and the school's automobile in the late teens and 1920s, shuttled Miss Livingston and students to various locales, including St. Thomas' Episcopal Church on Sunday mornings. Though most students walked up Garrison Forest Road to the nearby church, a lucky few rode. History teacher Dorothy Hall would determine who could ride based on injuries and lateness.

GARRISON FOREST ROARS INTO THE 1920s

GFS had firmly established several traditions by 1920. Students beyond the primary grades were divided into Light and Dark blue spirit teams—blue was Miss Livingston's favorite color—and graduating classes carried bouquets of blue cornflowers or Ragged Robins, the name also given to the yearbook and, in 1952, to Garrison Forest's a cappella student singing group. To pay for their yearbook and the first Garrison Forest class ring, the Class of 1920 hosted a fundraising dance at the Baltimore Country Club. Bob Eula's Orchestra provided the entertainment, and with a cover charge of $1 per couple, the class raised $100. At all school dances, the "four-inch rule" was strictly enforced, with chaperones making sure that young gentleman and ladies were situated far enough apart while dancing.

The dawn of a new decade brought a change to the role of women in the United States, a change mirrored at GFS. With the ratification of the 19th Amendment in 1920, women now had the right to vote and were venturing into the political arena. The new cultural mores of the "Roaring Twenties"—along with the era's shortened hemlines, bobbed hair, and no corsets—were helping to transform a woman's social and professional roles and opportunities. Girls' physical education was now an important part of school life, and Garrison Forest added programs for riding, tennis, track, and basketball. While competing against teachers and other schools such as Hannah More Academy, Oldfields School, and Roland Park Country School (RPCS), the girls could show their legs, albeit covered in dark stockings. These, along with bloomers and a sailor top, comprised the athletic uniform. Post-GFS or college, several Garrison graduates embraced the growing national trend and entered the workforce, typically as secretaries, nurses, social workers, or teachers.

The campus was also changing. Moncrieffe Hall, named for Miss Livingston's family because she eschewed the suggestion that it be named for her, opened in 1920 with classrooms and dormitory rooms. A gymnasium was built a year later and was used for physical education, basketball games (including raucous matches between the Lights and Darks), chapel services, and plays. While it was not officially a part of the GFS campus, a white house across Reisterstown Road became an auxiliary building in 1919. That year, the trustees rented the house when Rev. Smith, Miss Livingston's brother-in-law, retired from St. Thomas'. He and his wife moved into the

"Deanery," and Miss Livingston's mother, Esther Livingston, continued to live in Manor House until her death on June 21, 1921.[5]

In late winter 1923, Miss Livingston was in a car accident. Her recovery kept her away from school for most of the spring. In early 1925, Miss Livingston was hospitalized in New York after suffering injuries from another car accident. By December 28, 1925, she tendered her resignation to the trustees as school principal and as Treasurer of the Green Spring Valley School, Inc. While the Board recognized the school's "splendid accomplishments under her administration…and her expressed desire to be relieved of some of the burden and responsibility of the expanding activities of the school," they refused to accept Miss Livingston's resignation. They voted unanimously that she remain as principal and that a search would begin for an associate principal. No such position was ever filled during the remaining years of Miss Livingston's tenure.

In March 1928, Miss Livingston again suffered serious injuries from another car accident, this time in Pittsburgh. When she returned to her beloved campus and students, the change in leadership she had been seeking could no longer be delayed. Though enrollment by the 1928-29 year had reached 48 students (27 boarders and 21 day students) across the divisions (primary through twelfth grade), the school was running in the red. By June 1, 1928, Garrison Forest had a deficit of $34,765 and its campus was in need of repairs. During trustee meetings, there was talk of major renovations: converting the original stable and garage into classrooms for the primary department (soon to be called the Infantry), constructing a new stable, rewiring Manor House, upgrading the property's original drainage system, and installing fire-fighting equipment. All required funds that the school did not have.

TURNING OVER THE REINS

Mr. Shriver did not look far for Miss Livingston's replacement. He first approached Dorothy M. Hall, history teacher. Though Miss Hall would eventually retire in 1960 as assistant headmistress, she kindly refused Mr. Shriver's request in 1928. Next on his list was the newest member of the GFS faculty: Jean Gilmor Marshall, a young, former World War I Army nurse who coached field hockey and basketball at Garrison Forest. Mr. Shriver had long been acquainted with Miss Marshall, as her family, like

As the only school building for nearly a decade, Manor House was schoolhouse, dormitory, dining hall, recital hall, administrative offices, and the residence for Miss Livingston and her mother. Since then, Manor House has served the Garrison Forest community in many ways: as a gathering place, dormitory, infirmary, dining room, activity center, offices, and faculty residence, and the school store run by Clover "Kitty" Roulette since 1982. The heart of the campus, Manor House's distinctive brown-shingled exterior and welcoming, wide porch inspired the architectural vernacular for much of the campus.

Miss Livingston and George M. Shriver, President of the GFS Board from 1918-42. For the 1921 *Ragged Robin* yearbook dedication, a student penned a poem about Miss Livingston, which included the following verse:
"She is of the truest blue,
With ever a cheer for all,
She is a good sport all through,
Even though she is not tall.
With a kind word for every girl,
She starts us on the roll,
From the highest hair to the littlest curl,
She leads us toward our goal."

Miss Livingston posing on the Manor House porch.

the Shrivers, lived in the Green Spring Valley. She agreed to take on the job of headmistress on one condition: that her friend and colleague on the RPCS faculty, Nancy Jenkins Offutt, join her.[6] "With the valor of ignorance," Miss Offutt wrote, she and Miss Marshall accepted. By the end of December 1928, they had reached an agreement with the board: Miss Livingston would retire the following June, at which point they would begin their tenure as co-headmistresses.

To solve the school's financial crisis, Mr. Shriver and J. Sawyer Wilson, Jr., board secretary, proposed issuing $100,000 in bonds with the campus as collateral. Mr. Shriver held bonds totaling $26,000, while Mr. Wilson held $12,000 in bonds. Miss Livingston's original common stock was refunded in a $10,000 annuity, and both Miss Marshall and Miss Offutt each received $5,000 in The Green Spring Valley School, Inc. stock. Further, Mr. Shriver and Mr. Wilson each agreed to advance the school up to $8,000 to pay existing bank loans.

June 1929 marked the end of Miss Livingston's era as founding headmistress, though she continued her association with the school. During her first year of retirement, with the title of Principal Emerita, she lived in Manor House, where she kept a watchful eye and corresponded with alumnae, but did not involve herself heavily in the school's day-to-day activities.[7]

Both Miss Marshall and Miss Offutt had teaching but no administrative experience, and neither had ever been to a boarding school. Their first fall at GFS, they hosted the senior dance. With only six seniors in the class, the headmistresses also agreed to include the two members of the junior class and the faculty. As the evening wore on, it became obvious that two of the boys in attendance had been drinking, and one was sitting—uninvited—on the lap of the Latin teacher. The boys were asked to leave and did so with little incident. The dance proceeded, and at the end of the evening, Miss Marshall and Miss Offutt, wearing long white gloves, stood at the door of Manor House to shake the hands of each student and her date.

What happened afterward left a lasting impression on the fledgling headmistresses. "The next morning Miss Livingston was told by a friend that the whole road was littered with whiskey bottles and that there had been a terrible drunken brawl," recalled Miss Offutt. Miss Livingston sent for the young headmistresses, who, after explaining that it had not been "a drunken brawl," told Miss Livingston that they found the whole incident rather funny. Miss Livingston then pulled out a pint of whiskey that had been left on the campus and told them that she failed to find the humor in the situation. "We should have asked her to come down and

receive with us," admitted Miss Offutt more than 50 years later. "As you can well imagine, it was not the happiest situation for her… to see two young women coming in there to take over. I don't really feel that I knew her, for which I'm very sorry, but she must have been a person of vision and imagination and everything else or she wouldn't have done what she did [for Garrison Forest.]"

On November 1, 1957, Garrison Forest dedicated the portrait of Miss Livingston, which now hangs in the Manor House hallway. At the unveiling, Miss Marshall spoke of the legacy of the founding headmistress: "For such a long time, we have been looking forward to this day when the school would own a portrait of its founder, when we could say to the youngest student as well as to the alumnae of all years, 'This is Miss Livingston. Because of her, we are here.' Continuity is a strong force. Nowhere is it more important than in the life of a school when deep loyalties are born and young ships set their course for what may be their whole life's journey. It is good at last Mary Moncrieffe Livingston will be here always, not as a name, but as a person, joining our day with hers and with the many, many days to come, deepening for us the dear sense of belonging, strengthening the pride that we feel in our school's past, the confidence with which we look ahead."

Charles Garland, President of the Board, Miss Marshall, Edith Ney '14, and Miss Offutt at the dedication of Miss Livingston's portrait.

Riding on campus in 1923.

From 1910 until 1969, Garrison Forest students were required to attend Sunday services at St. Thomas' Church. The historic church continues to be the location of the Baccalaureate service for seniors and their families.

GARRISON FOREST AND ST. THOMAS'

Garrison Forest School, though founded without any religious affiliation, has enjoyed an abiding connection with St. Thomas' Church for generations. The relationship with the Episcopal church began, quite literally, as family, when Miss Livingston's sister, Esther Livingston, married St. Thomas' Rector, Rev. Hobart Smith, in 1889. (He had begun his 35-year tenure at St. Thomas' the previous year.) Miss Livingston, her mother, and brother were frequent visitors to the Rectory and the historic church, which was founded in 1742.

Many of the congregants in the late 1800s and early 1900s advocated for a local school. Their concerns did not fall on deaf ears with Rev. and Mrs. Smith. Under his leadership, St. Thomas' expanded its parish school, which supported the community until his retirement in 1918. (Parish and school records indicate that Miss Livingston was not part of the faculty or administration of any parish-sponsored school.) Both Smiths were strong proponents of Miss Livingston establishing a school in the Green Spring Valley—and strong supporters of Garrison Forest. While it is assumed that Mrs. Smith's frail health kept her from attending school events, Rev. Smith was a frequent attendee at school functions. It is unclear if he formally held the position of GFS chaplain (he was chaplain for McDonogh School for 25 years), but he was a popular member of the school community, even garnering a yearbook dedication in 1924.

Every Sunday, Miss Livingston and her boarders attended services at St. Thomas'. Margaret Marees Wills '24 wrote of continual lateness for church, often the result of excessive primping and outfit changes. For decades, boarders continued to walk to church, presumably slightly behind schedule, but buoyed by the hope of social interaction. "We used to groan, but I

liked going every Sunday, hoping to see local Baltimore boys there!" recalled Mary Matthiessen Wheelwright '43. In 1945, Miss Marshall and GFS Choir director Roberta Glanville arranged for the GFS choir to sing on a monthly basis in lieu of the St. Thomas' choir. When Rev. Henry Rightor, St. Thomas' Rector from 1957-65, established a family service at 9:30 a.m. to relieve congestion at the 11:00 a.m. service, Garrison Forest students began attending the new service.

If a student was Roman Catholic, the school arranged for her to attend Sunday morning Mass at a local Catholic church, typically Miss Offutt's church, St. Charles Borromeo Roman Catholic Church in Pikesville. Katherine Condon '57, one of a handful of Catholics in the mid-1950s who attended Mass with Miss Offutt, drove the GFS station wagon to church one Sunday after Miss Offutt's attempts to start the car's finicky engine failed. "Having acquired my Tennessee license at the early age of 14 (with a bit of family finagling), I asked if I might give it a try," said Katherine. "I was delighted to receive not only praises but also the great privilege of becoming Miss Offutt's Sunday morning-go-to-church chauffeur! I will always remember her sweet smile of relief and her entirely unwarranted faith in my driving skills."

Students also were required to attend a candlelit Vespers service on Sunday evenings in the Little Gym. Beginning in 1958, a student-led, voluntary Wednesday night Vespers was added. On January 11, 1959, Vespers was held in the school's new chapel, inaugurating the rustic, yet elegant building, which had been a long-held dream of the deeply spiritual Miss Marshall and Miss Offutt. Headmaster Archibald "Tad" R. Montgomery III, embracing his predecessors' belief that God is best found on an individual basis, added the position of school chaplain. (Prior to this, it is assumed that a member of the St. Thomas' clergy served this role.) In1965, Rev. Emily Preston, a recently ordained United Church of Christ minister, became the first official GFS chaplain. She helped to plan weekly chapel services, presided over Chapel during alumnae and parent events, and taught the religion and ethics courses. In subsequent years, the position has been filled by clergy who have been members of the St. Thomas' staff and from other Protestant denominations.

In 1969, with students clamoring for more academic and social freedom, Garrison Forest no longer mandated regular attendance at St. Thomas' or for Sunday evening Vespers, though the latter requirement would be re-instated by the GFS student-led Chapel Committee during the 1970s. The always-voluntary Wednesday evening Vespers at GFS was well attended, though, offering student talks and prayer.

The 1980s brought more change to the school's formal, Christian-based religious programming. Vespers attendance was no longer required, and in 1985, the morning assembly Prayers had a name change to Morning Meeting. In 1988, the GFS board's Education Committee tried to revive a religious program—to mixed reviews—through a Thursday morning, ecumenical service during Morning Meeting, which included prayers, hymns, and an introduction to different religions. A year later, the program was scrapped in favor of a more informal program to reflect Garrison Forest's growing religious diversity.

The school's lasting connection with St. Thomas' endures through the annual Baccalaureate Service. The earliest recorded service at the church was on May 28, 1922, two days before Commencement. For nearly a century, graduating seniors have filed into St. Thomas' sanctuary to raise their voices and reflect on the speaker's challenge of a future beyond GFS. After the close of an inspirational service, students continue the tradition of posing for photos with classmates, teachers, and family within yards of the final resting place of Mary Moncrieffe Livingston.

An 1896 photo with members of the St. Thomas' Vestry (first row, left to right: George N. Moale, Rev. Hobart Smith, Charles Morton Stewart; second row, left to right: Samuel M. Shoemaker, II, John McHenry, William Fell Johnson). McHenry and Stewart were founding members of The Green Spring Valley School, Inc.

Mr. Shriver addressed each graduating class, pictured here with the Class of 1939. French Shriver Foster '42 recalled her grandfather's habit when speaking in public: "He would put his hand in his pocket and jingle his pocket change. Classmates teased me that I should get some of that change, but you never asked him for anything. He'd turn his head and change the subject, but he was always very generous with us. And he would do anything for Garrison Forest."

GEORGE M. SHRIVER

"It's really his school more than it is anybody's," Miss Offutt said in 1981, words that reflected the abiding gratitude and friendship that Miss Marshall and she enjoyed with George McLean Shriver, and he with them and Garrison Forest School. During his unmatched tenure as president of the Garrison Forest board from 1918 until his death in 1942, Mr. Shriver worked hand-in-hand with the headmistresses to transform the school from a local day school with a handful of boarders into a nationally recognized independent school with a thriving residential program. Shriver Hall, built in 1939, bears his name, and his numerous descendents and relatives have attended and taught at GFS, including daughter Helen Shriver Moore '15 who taught domestic arts in the late 1910s and early 1920s.

His association with the school began in 1911 or 1912, when he and his wife, Elizabeth Chism Shriver, enrolled their daughters, Helen and Elizabeth "Tibs" Shriver Moore '19. In 1918, Mr. Shriver succeeded Laurence Miller as board president, and for 24 years Mr. Shriver's quiet, gracious manner and generosity sustained Garrison Forest and shaped its future. He selected Miss Livingston's replacements and footed the bill for campus improvements and countless expenditures, large and small, among them the school's first automobile in 1919, an Auburn purchased for $330 and nicknamed "Reddy" by the students. He also encouraged his many business contacts across the U.S. to enroll their daughters.

"My grandfather was more action than words," recalled George M. Shriver III. "He was an imposing figure, not physically, but through his presence." George M. Shriver was the son of a Presbyterian minister, and as the senior vice president of the Baltimore & Ohio (B&O) Railroad, he was one of the country's experts in railroad finance. As such, he had plenty of wisdom to offer, but only when requested. "He would never offer advice nor would he raise his voice," his grandson noted. His soft conversational tone became known as the "Shriver murmur."

Mr. Shriver's investments in Garrison Forest typically followed a pattern: He would borrow money from the First National Bank of Maryland, of which he was a director; lend the sum to GFS in return for interest-bearing bonds; and then pledge the bonds as collateral to the bank for the school's loan. While it is impossible to calculate the value in today's dollars of his 25-plus year investment in the school—he kept his own books at home and kept his support quiet—it is clear that his generosity allowed Garrison Forest to maintain and move forward throughout his tenure. In 1941, the headmistresses decided that they had to have a new gym. Miss Marshall and Miss Offutt shared their idea with Mr. Shriver, to which he replied, "Um-hum." Arm-in-arm with Mr. Shriver, the two women, along with his daughter Tibs, who often accompanied her father on his GFS visits to "keep [him] from simply giving everything he had," noted Miss Offutt, showed him the exact spot where the gym should be built. He agreed to the plans, and the next day the headmistresses had a hole dug. Vice president J. Sawyer Wilson, Jr. was not as amenable to the idea. After the women called Mr. Shriver to ask if they needed to fill the hole, he said he would take care of it. Mr. Shriver proceeded to purchase Mr. Wilson's GFS stock, and as Miss Offutt recalled, "Mr. Wilson was happy…and the building was built." The blueprints for both the gym and Shriver Hall remained in Mr. Shriver's roll-top desk until his death.

In October 1943, Miss Offutt wrote to Charles M. Shriver, who succeeded his father as GFS board president, with a check to repay George Shriver's many loans to the school: "Neither of us will ever forget that the bleaker and more desperate our prospects became, the more generously [Mr. Shriver] thought of excuses for us, the more sure he became of ultimate success. This school is certainly the living expression of his courage and generosity and of a faith by which he always saw the main objective, above or beneath or around the obstacle of the moment. I wish so much that he were here to-day [sic], and yet I feel that he will never go too far away from all of us…I can see him smiling, I can hear him saying, 'Well, now, very good, very good.' " Since 1950, the Shriver Award has been presented annually at Commencement by vote of faculty to the senior who best exemplifies a broad range of leadership.

Following the construction of Meadowood in 1957, the school created a pond on campus. In 1975, the pond was named "Moore's Landing" in honor of Charles J. Moore, the husband of Elizabeth "Tibs" Shriver Moore '19, George Shriver's daughter. While a student, she often drove her pony cart to school, and after learning to drive at age 13 by sitting on a pillow, she frequently drove her father, who did not drive, to GFS for meetings. Miss Offutt wrote that while Miss Marshall and she "walked around the campus with Mr. Shriver building more 'stately mansions,' Tibs [a trustee from 1950-88] noticed the sagging rain spout, heavy with leaves, the leaking hot water faucet, the broken limb that could fall in the next storm…Her judgment was always true."

Alsenborn, the Shriver farm in Pikesville, was the site of year-end picnics for students. The swimming pool was particularly popular, but only "if it had been a warm May," chuckled French Foster, who started at the school in the fall of 1928 when she was four, because, "GFS needed students and my grandfather had to fill it up." On the weekend before exams, boarders would come to the Shriver farm for a swim and a picnic lunch served by B&O waiters.

SPIRITED TRADITIONS

White dresses and Ragged Robins: a Garrison Forest tradition.

THE
CLAS
The
Party w
display
and of
whole
gether

Adele Smith Simmons '59, editor of the school newspaper, *The Blueprint*, in 1958-59, reflected on the school motto in her editorial, *"Esse Quam Videri:"*

Perhaps the greatest drawback of living in the close contact of a boarding school is the feeling that each individual must make her actions and thoughts conform to those of others. This should not be so, yet many without thinking allow themselves to be poured into a fixed mold where they remain until they are firmly cast into a figure identical to that of their contemporaries who were once molded in the same way. For a few this figure is an ideal, but a vast majority are unhappy, yet they lack both the courage and the spark necessary needed to break their mold and create their own figure. The few with strength of character either break the mold and emerge as individuals, or, better still, never permit themselves to be poured into it. These are real people for they have their own ideas and are not just puppets.

By pretending to be something you aren't and can never really be, you waste the most important years of your life, for during the years of a secondary education you create a set of standards to be followed throughout your life. It is at this time that you can discover and freely pursue your own interests and begin an extremely important period of questioning and testing the fundamental beliefs that had once been taken for granted. You decide whether these basic faiths are right, and if not, what is.

Your ideals can only be discovered through your own thoughts and efforts, for the answer is always there, but for each person it is hidden in a different place, yet if you allow yourself to be ruled by actions and thoughts that are not your own, your original ideas will have neither the opportunity to develop nor the chance to be tested. You must not be afraid of letting these ideas crystallize, for it is only when they acquire form and shape that you can examine them closely and judge them for what they are worth.

Act yourself, for only then can you find true satisfaction and peace of mind and at the same time take the greatest advantage of what is offered to you. Most individuals are happier and more relaxed while behaving in a natural way, yet many continue to forfeit this and copy others as if to cover up for something. If any friends are gained in this way, they may not be your friends with your beliefs, but friends of your artificial self. If you act in a way which you truly believe to be right, you will find your own friends and the place in the community which only you can fill, for the thoughts and ideas expressed will be your own individual ones, and not those of someone else.

Therefore you must not be afraid of yourself as an individual, but be thankful that you possess the qualities which allow you to be one. You should not cover up what you really are by trying to imitate another person, but stand firm in your beliefs and take advantage of every opportunity that will prepare you for the future.

ESSE QUAM VIDERI — TO BE RATHER THAN TO SEEM

When Miss Livingston chose the motto of *Esse Quam Videri* — To Be Rather Than To Seem, the words expressed far more than her hopes and vision for her then-fledgling school. They reflected her warmth, simplicity, and sincerity—character traits she sought to inculcate within each student. At the time, though, her choice of a motto championing authenticity of character was hardly unique. By the early 1900s, dozens of private schools, colleges, and organizations worldwide had chosen *Esse Quam Videri* as a motto, including the State of North Carolina.[1]

Whether Miss Livingston knew of the motto from her own education and reading or admired the motto of another school, the legacy of her choice far outweighs its origin. *Esse Quam Videri* continues to inspire generations at Garrison Forest. On the occasion of the school's 25th anniversary, the 1935 *Ragged Robin* yearbook stated, "… We hope that… *Esse Quam Videri* will become more and more our keynote and goal until it is an obvious part of the personality of every Garrison Forest girl her life long."

Clinton Arrowood, GFS music and art history faculty member and illustrator, included the motto on several of his book covers. Here, the motto is on the top of the mirror frame.

Since at least 1978, the senior class has donned silly outfits to practice processing for Commencement.

COMMENCEMENT

Garrison Forest held its first Commencement in 1914, graduating two college-bound seniors (out of a two-member class). Over the years, the location of the Commencement ceremony has been in the Big Gym, on Lochinvar's lawn, in Garland Theater, and even one year at the edge of Moore's Landing, the pond near Robinswood. Commencements since the 1980s have been held in the courtyard, with school closing activities in the Middle School and Lower Division. The styles of the white graduation dresses have changed over the years, but the tradition of the senior class posing in front of the white clapboard Senior House has not.

Clinton Arrowood

SCHOOL RING

The Class of 1920 created the first GFS school ring, raising the funds to pay for their rings through a dance at the Baltimore Country Club. In the ensuing years, the ring design has changed, but not the tradition of juniors anxiously awaiting the giving of their rings by the seniors. Legend once held that the first junior to receive her ring would be the last to marry, and the last to receive hers would be the first to marry. Other classes wore them with the flame on the lamp of the school seal facing toward them to symbolize knowledge flowing inward. Upon graduating, the ring's flame would be placed outward. Other rules of engagement required one's senior ring sister to "unlock," or turn, the ring for the first time so the crest faced up before others could turn the ring. In 1989, the Class of 1990 sponsored the first Ring Dance for juniors, seniors, and their dates, a tradition that has continued. "It is more than a ring," noted President of the School Anisah Imani '09 in her 2009 Commencement speech. "It is a physical connection to the school and all the memories created here that every Garrison Girl is able to carry with her, no matter how far she travels from [school]."

RAGGED ROBIN

The term "Ragged Robin" applies to three longstanding GFS traditions—the school flower, the yearbook, and the student a cappella group—each of which is an equally beloved part of the school's rich history and indomitable spirit. (Illustration, left, by Carrington Dame Hooper '54.)

In 1952, students created the Ragged Robins a cappella singing group, whose audition-based membership of juniors and seniors performs light classics, folk, and popular music for on- and off-campus events, including state competitions. A cappella groups reached their zenith at Garrison Forest in the early 1980s with four separate, audition-based singing groups: the Flappers (freshmen); the doo-wop Pink Minks (sophomores); and the juniors' Footnotes. At the time, the Ragged Robins was for seniors only. In 1963, tone-deaf students formed the Shredded Tweets, an on-again, off-again, tongue-in-cheek, anti-Ragged Robins singing group whose motto was, "You name it, we'll ruin it."

Presumably, the blue cornflower or bachelor's button, *Centaurea cyanus*, was chosen by Miss Livingston. Graduating seniors during her era wore white dresses and carried arm bouquets of the simple blossoms. The tradition continued of Commencement bouquets wrapped in flowing blue ribbons, which the school called "Ragged Robins." Actually, the Ragged Robin, *Lychnis flos-cuculi*, is not a cornflower at all, though like the cornflower, it is naturalized as a wildflower in the Northeast. (Illustration, right, of Ragged Robins by Bee Shriver Kant '54.)

Also named *Ragged Robin*, the earliest yearbook of record was published in 1920. Several decades later, the Class of 1965 created a senior page in the yearbook for "classmate" Susan Fledgling Fremont. Nearly every word on Susan's page is a clue to her fictitious status. Her "classmates" went on to create an elaborate post-GFS life for her in the *Alumnae Magazine*.

SUSAN FLEDGLING FREMONT

"*Monie,*" "*Suchey,*" "*Freeda*"

DODGE CITY, KANSAS

Entered 1957

"*Well, General, we have not had many dead cavalrymen lying about lately*"

President of the Russian Club . . . Lower School escapades with Dodie . . . Name on more school documents than any other student . . . On every squad . . . "That's Lynnie lectures" . . . "I am, too" . . . "Call me indescribable" . . . Freudian discussions with Martha . . . Thanksgiving with Seggerman . . . Ghost writer . . . The missing link . . . Giving Thanksgiving with Seggerman . . . Trick-or-treating with Miss White . . . That lost weekend blues . . . Private conferences with Mr. Watts . . . Early admissions at Beechtree U . . . Biology Throwing marshmallows at Laura Sims in Greek class . . . First fifth-grader in Riding Club more folk art . . . Student government member for eight years . . . To be and not to seem . . . with Henderson . . . Brother is All-American pass-receiver on Yale football team . . . 9th, 10th, 11th, 12th . . . matter expert . . . Typing lessons from Po . . . Vague, evasive, non-descript . . . Anti-

Always saying: M A

LIGHT BLUE AND DARK BLUE

Miss Livingston's selection of the school's colors was simple: blue was her favorite color. Garrison Forest's Light Blue and Dark Blue quickly became more than just ribbon colors to adorn graduation bouquets. The earliest records of sorting students into spirit teams dubbed "Lights" and "Darks" dates back to 1920. Legacies (siblings, cousins, granddaughters, and other family members) receive the same designation as the first GFS family member, and faculty and staff are sorted as well, with the notable exception of the Head of School, who must remain unbiased.

Since the beginning of the spirit team tradition, students have earned points for their team through service and leadership, as elected officers and behind the scenes, as well as through spirited Light/Dark athletic competitions and official Spirit Day events, which began in the early 1970s. A few decades earlier, GFS students displayed a Light or Dark blue patch on school blazers and riders draped Light and Dark blue blankets over their horses. At Commencement, the winning spirit team with the highest number of points is announced to great cheers by Lights and Darks. Since 1984, the school has awarded the Elizabeth G. Brown Spirit Award to the most spirited class, an honor named for Miss Brown, who kept track of all spirit points from 1938-70. In the 1980s, the elected spirit captains began decorating their tunics to wear on Spirit Days, a tradition individual team members have since adopted. Students personalize their tunics, and don hats, wigs, and other costume accessories to show their spirit and showcase their team.

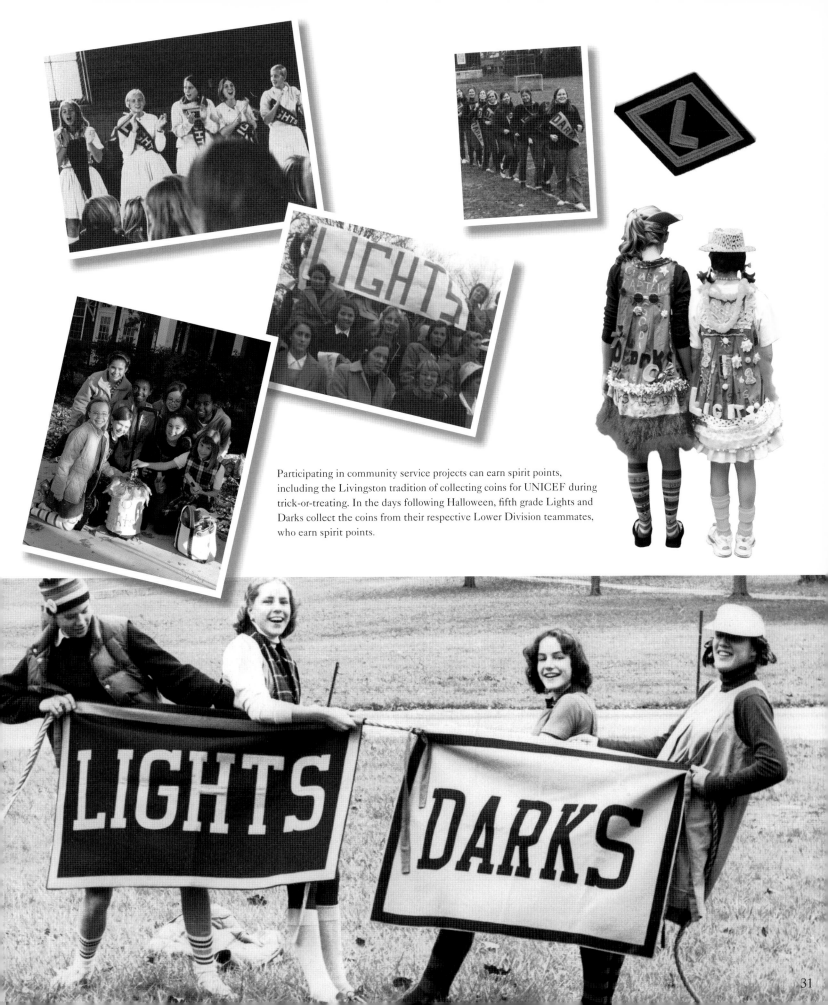

Participating in community service projects can earn spirit points, including the Livingston tradition of collecting coins for UNICEF during trick-or-treating. In the days following Halloween, fifth grade Lights and Darks collect the coins from their respective Lower Division teammates, who earn spirit points.

ALMA MATER

Hail, Gladdening Light.

Our lamp of wisdom, Hail!

Shine with a radiance

Which can never fail.

Illumined by thy rays.

Must thus our motto gleam,

And show our desire

"To be and not to seem."

Polished and fitted true,

May each to each stand fast,

Firm as the stones

In Temple corners cast.

Strong and enduring be

Our love and loyalty

For School and for Comrades

And for Victory.

FAREWELL TO THE FOREST

Thou forest broad and sweeping,
Fair work of nature's God,
Of all my joy and weeping,
The consecrate abode.
Yon world deceiving ever,
Murmurs in vain alarm.
O, might I wander never
From thy protecting arms.
O, might I wander never
From thy protecting arms.

Who rightly scans thy beauty,
A solemn word shall read
Of love of truth and duty,
Our hope in time of need.
And I have read them often,
Those words so true and clear,
What heart that would not soften,
Thy wisdom to revere,
What heart that would not soften,
Thy wisdom to revere.

ALMA MATER

Lois Bryan Wood '20, one of the original students in 1910, could not recall exactly if Miss Livingston wrote the words to the Garrison Forest alma mater or if the students helped, but she was quite clear on the selection of the tune from Miss Livingston's favorite Episcopal hymn, "God, the Omnipotent" by Alexis Lvov (1798-1870). Each morning, Miss Livingston would assemble all her charges in the Manor House hallway for prayers and to sing the alma mater. After announcements, students would recess to the "Triumphal March" from Verdi's opera *Aida*, chosen because it was the only tune the accompanist and French teacher, Mademoiselle Gilles, knew well. The alma mater continues to be sung regularly as a part of Morning Meeting, with exuberant emphasis placed on the last line of the second verse: VIC-TOR-Y!

COLLEGE WALL

Each year, since the early 1990s, the painted cinderblock walls of the Senior Room in Marshall-Offutt become a multicolored mosaic as seniors accept college admission offers. Each senior paints a brick in her soon-to-be-college's logo and colors, and each summer, it is painted over to await the next class.

Garrison Forest School

Directory

1978 - 79

THE SEAL

A precursor to the Garrison Forest School seal may be found on a letter to Anne Jouett Davis '30, written by Miss Livingston on June 23, 1929. On the letterhead, the French motto, *"Si Je Puis"*—"If I Can"—unfurls beneath a man holding a snake and a spear, a modification of the Livingston family's coat-of-arms. Her version, though, does not appear on any known GFS yearbooks or other publications during her tenure. In spring 1929, the official Garrison Forest seal made its debut on the cover of the *Ragged Robin* yearbook. The seal depicted a tree upholding a lamp, the symbol of education, with Garrison Forest's motto emblazoned beneath. In 1985, the current seal was created, retaining the tree, lamp, and motto. The large tree in the modern-era seal resembles a White Oak, *Quercus alba*. Known for its majestic stature, wide branches, and longevity, the White Oak is the state tree of Maryland. A prominent specimen may be found near the school's Reisterstown Road entrance.

Written by Miss Livingston in 1929, the letter at right urged student Anne Jouett Davis to enjoy her upcoming steamer trip to Europe. Miss Livingston describes a post-graduation alumnae luncheon and encourages Anne, who apparently was considering not returning to school in the fall, to return: "We want you very much, and I am sure you will find another year here will mean much to you…My dear child, have a very happy summer, keep well, and come back to G.F.S. Oct. first and tell us all about it!! Don't forget me, and send me some postcards often. Much love always from your affectionate friend, Mary M. Livingston."

Sunday. June 23

The Garrison Forest School
Green Spring Valley
Garrison, Maryland

Dearest Anne Jouett.

I was truly much pleased to have you

FACULTY FOLLIES

Pictured (left), the self-effacing Mr. O'Neill, a Motown fan, cuts a rug with English teacher Carol Peabody in a spoof of a popular TV dancing show for the 2008 Faculty Follies. The first Faculty Follies was on May 3, 1972, when the GFS faculty and staff surprised the school with a series of skits written, produced, and performed by teachers, administrators, and staff. Created as a morale booster following the controversial, aborted campus move and merger with St. Timothy's in 1971, the first Faculty Follies poked good-hearted fun at Garrison Forest and its personalities. Every few years since, another Faculty Follies debuts to the delight of the students. Pictured far left are (left to right) Mr. Montgomery, business manager J. Sawyer Wilson III, and teacher Richard Watts performing a skit before the days of Faculty Follies.

NEW GIRL AND BIG SISTER/LITTLE SISTER

For nearly 80 years, being new at Garrison Forest meant being part of New Girl initiation. Early traditions included New Girls "singing, dancing, wriggling, and gurgling at the command of the almighty old girls," (1935 *Ragged Robin*) and making the beds of the "old" girls. By the mid-20th century, New Girls and often, new teachers, dressed in a senior-devised theme, using the blue tunic and belt as the basis for the ensemble. In the mid-1990s, the tradition shifted into an expanded Big Sister/Little Sister program in recognition of Garrison Forest's increasingly diverse population with cultural traditions that did not include, nor embrace, initiation rituals. The oldest and youngest students in each division are matched as Big Sister and Little Sister and participate in activities designed to create community.

The "Batman tunic," 1985.

Big Sister/Little Sister.

Seniors chose each year's New Girl theme. Costumes ran the gamut from bees, dogs, togas, and Hawaiian hula dancers to beauty queens and superheroes, but each had a common thread: The GFS tunic and belt had to be part of the attire. Sometimes, New Girl costumes echoed the themes of the day. In 1959, at the height of the Cold War, the New Girls were the "new missiles" and the seniors were the "generals."

New Girl initiation week typically began with Senior Skits and ended with New Girl Skits, during which seniors welcomed the newest Garrison girls with handmade hats proclaiming their newly obtained "Old Girl" status.

JUNIOR/SENIOR PICNIC AND SENIOR ESCAPE

Miss Marshall and Miss Offutt helped to quell spring fever by cancelling classes for a day for the junior and senior classes. At the Junior/Senior Picnic, the classes and several teachers would enjoy relaxing, recreation, and a picnic lunch, typically held at the nearby home of a Garrison Forest family. Pictured right is the 1953-54 Junior/Senior Picnic at White Hall near Annapolis, the home of Kitsie Scarlett Burnett '54. In 1969, the seniors planned the first Senior Escape Day, during which the seniors "kidnapped" a handful of selected faculty members for a day of off-campus fun. Until the mid-1980s, Senior Escape Day was a surprise to everyone except the seniors. The "kidnapping" tradition continues, but now faculty members get advance warning.

1989 Senior Escape

Head of Middle School and artist Steve McManus rewards students with a hand-drawn merit slip (left and bottom).

Digging weeds, 1940s.

MERITS/DEMERITS

A longstanding tradition at independent schools, the demerit system typically doles out punishment to student rule-breakers. At Garrison Forest in the Marshall-Offutt era, tardiness, uniform infractions, and other less-than-desirable behaviors had consequences unique to the punisher. The practical and penny-pinching Miss Marshall had students work off demerits by picking up stones in the riding fields, or with table knives in hand, dig out weeds. The philosophical Miss Offutt required that students copy chapter after chapter out of the Bible for a more reflective punishment. Students in the 21st century attend detention after a few infractions, and merits are given for good behavior or deeds.

French teacher Mary K. Boyd and her ever-present and
exceedingly well-behaved German Shepherd.

JEAN G. MARSHALL AND NANCY J. OFFUTT
CO-HEADMISTRESSES, 1929-1960

By the close of Miss Marshall's and Miss Offutt's first year, Garrison Forest had shrunk its deficit to slightly less than $11,000 through refinancing, and the school was soon able to begin much-needed campus renovations. The original stable was converted into classrooms for a formal primary department for girls and boys ages four through fourth grade, which assumed the title of "The Infantry" as the result of a contest. The stable's second-story hayloft was renovated for art and music classrooms. (The smell of hay lingered for years on damp days.) A new garage and stable also were built, and one year later, the school purchased two additional acres.

Garrison Forest's financial woes, though, were far from over. As the impact of the Great Depression spread from Wall Street to Main Street, and banks closed and breadlines formed, schools across the country experienced significant drops in enrollment. Many families could no longer afford the tuition for private education. In 1928-29, 21 day scholars and 27 boarders were enrolled. By the following year, enrollment had dropped to eight day scholars and 23 boarders. [Records list only upper grade enrollment, though the coed nursery through primary department existed at the time.] "Disaster," Miss Offutt wrote, "like a sullen fog, hung over the country and, of course, Garrison Forest."

Mary Purdy, hired at age 16 in 1929 to work in the pantry, recalled a Depression-era visit to the GFS kitchen by Miss Offutt to inform the staff that the school could not afford to pay them. "We worked for several weeks during the Depression without pay," said Mrs. Purdy, who retired from GFS in 1980 and remains the longest-tenured faculty or staff member in the school's history. "Miss Offutt came and said, 'If you all will just stick with us, we promise we will make it up to you.'" When asked if the staff received their back pay, Mrs. Purdy smiled, "Most of it," she chuckled.

"A kind of euphoria must have possessed us, even when we did hide under the hedge to escape the milkman and the sausage man whose bills we could not pay," reflected Miss Offutt in 1956. In July 1930, Rev. Philip Jensen, Rector at St. Thomas' Church and a GFS trustee, telephoned Miss

Miss Marshall (left) and Miss Offutt (right) at their desk with George Shriver's portrait watching over them.

Miss Offutt and Miss Marshall.

Miss Marshall and Miss Offutt's penny-pinching included Miss Marshall pruning trees and both women painting school furniture. Exceedingly charming, they convinced the seniors that it was a privilege to return to campus early each fall to assist with the painting.

In 1929, 16-year-old Mary Purdy joined the GFS staff. She retired 51 years later as head of housekeeping. Her sister, Carlene Scott, served GFS from 1979 to 2007.

Offutt to say that he had heard a rumor that the school would not be opening in the fall. "I believe that we would have heard, if it were true," was her stunned response. "That's all I want to know," came Dr. Jensen's kind reply. "I will deny it." Miss Offutt recounted that she never imagined that Garrison Forest could close. "I can still remember my frightened, desolate feeling, as I hung up the receiver," she wrote. "It was a July day, but the house was suddenly cold, and I remember it was raining."

It quickly became clear that financial oversight was not the strong suit of the two young women. During one of their first board meetings, George Shriver called for their financial report. Miss Offutt proceeded to explain that they "seemed to have lost roughly $10,000." Mr. Shriver cleared his throat, his habit when at a loss for words. He then remarked that the missing funds must be partly due to uncollected debt, to which Miss Offutt replied, that "true…we did lose money because people couldn't pay it, but most of the [$10,000] was lost because we spent it and didn't have it." After that meeting, Mr. Shriver arranged for someone else to keep the books and allow the women—or "the girls" as he affectionately called them—to concentrate on the business of educating students and inspiring faculty.

Their charms, formidable when combined, helped them weather and deflect many a potential situation. After Easter break in 1932, Miss Marshall and Miss Offutt were to meet several students in New York's Pennsylvania Station for the 12:40 p.m. train back to Baltimore. At 12:30 p.m., there was no sign of the headmistresses, nor had any tickets been purchased, also their responsibility. At one minute before the train's scheduled departure, Miss Marshall and Miss Offutt rushed down to the platform, each carrying a window-box full of yellow pansies. They asked a father and grandfather of two GFS students—until that moment, the men were strangers to each other—if they had any money. The men handed over all their cash and coin, and the women bustled the students onto the train. The gentlemen then turned to each other and suggested that they go enjoy a drink, only to discover that each was now without any cash.

During a routine fire inspection of the third floor of Moncrieffe Hall, where students lived, the fire inspector opened the door marked "Exit" only to find a broom closet. The story goes that he then turned to his guide, Miss Offutt, and stated the obvious: "This is a broom closet." She replied, "It's quite all right. All the girls know that it is a broom closet."

GROWING IN THE LEAN YEARS

"Miss Marshall and Miss Offutt had an incredible capacity to accept into their school all the families who wanted GFS for their daughters, and they shared a burning desire to educate these girls, priorities which greatly overshadowed the families' ability to pay," explained Courtney Garland Iglehart '48, former GFS trustee. "The faith that 'all would be well' was deeply rooted in both of them. How they got away with owing so many merchants for so long during the Depression and World War II is a tribute to their ingenuity, smiles, and sense of humor." Kitty McLane Hoffman '37, former director of riding, summed up the Marshall-Offutt years: "The place ran on charm."

One such example is the story of how Miss Offutt managed to solve a local telephone strike singlehandedly—or at least remedy the situation in Garrison Forest's favor. She and Miss Marshall had acquired one of the first phone numbers in the Pikesville area. Telephone strikes were common, however, which would impede students and parents from reaching each other via the headmistresses' phone. Miss Offutt's course of action involved wrapping up a box of the finest chocolates and delivering them to the telephone company. When she arrived, she expressed great sympathy for their situation and agreed that they should have increased wages. Lo and behold, Garrison Forest's phone service was restored before she returned to campus.

The school was desperate to fill spots during the early 1930s. In 1931, the senior class only had three members, all boarders. The Infantry helped to increase enrollment, and with the help of Suzanne White Whitman, neighbor and the first head of the riding department, GFS began recruiting from a wider geographical region than Maryland and its border states. Within one year, total enrollment rose from 31 to 82 students.

While formal scholarship funds did not yet exist in the school's budget, the headmistresses allowed students to attend at discounted rates, with one student being granted "free scholarship for…two years." Such had presumably been the practice at Garrison Forest, but in 1931, in an effort to stretch an already thread-thin operating budget, the board kindly requested that the women try to find a way to accept as many full-paying students as possible.[8] Enrollment continued to increase each year throughout the headmistresses' 30-year tenure, with only a one-year dip during World War II. By the start of 1945-46, with Garrison Forest and the rest of the country celebrating the end of the war, the school welcomed 178 students with 90 boarders from throughout the Mid-Atlantic and the Northeast states, as well as Georgia, Illinois, North Carolina, and Wisconsin.

Before moving to Evenlode, their residence just off campus grounds, Miss Marshall and Miss Offutt lived in Manor House, a building whose plumbing, and sometimes the men who fixed it, were less than reliable. One day before school opened, the headmistresses were painting furniture and waiting for a plumber to return and finish the half-completed job of unclogging the pipes. A staff member announced that a man was here to see them. "The plumber!" said Miss Offutt. "Let him wait!" After 45 minutes, the staff member returned and said that perhaps they should see the gentleman. "You mean the plumber?" Miss Offutt asked. "No, he's not the plumber... I think he is a parent." Miss Marshall quickly flew upstairs to change, and Miss Offutt, still in paint-splattered blue jeans, went to greet the father by saying, "I thought you were the plumber." Miss Offutt ordered the kitchen to bring three Scotch highballs, "good and strong," which arrived when Miss Marshall did. By the second round of drinks, the father was slapping his thigh, saying, "Best damn school I ever knew."

"We needed students so badly that we took a child who was… just plain allergic to all schools, even Garrison. The watchman cheerfully reported [that] he had seen a student clad in a polo coat over pajamas and carrying her shoes in her hand, slide down the Manor House trellis and take to the fields in the dawn's early light. We formed a kind of posse to hunt down the fugitive. Just north of school, there was an old abandoned house. I went into the house feeling that kind of delicious fright that stimulates you, imagining that she was somewhere in the shadows watching me…I thought I heard a sound. The light of day was behind me beyond the open door; in front, there was shuttered twilight. 'Come out,' I called, trembling. 'I know you are there.' There was a sound of shuffling and from behind the stair case appeared a dilapidated-looking character, male, very dirty and just as frightened as I was…I said, 'You can go back, you're not the right one.'"
—Miss Offutt

Even with a boarding and day program bursting at the seams, the headmistresses apparently did not adhere to strict limits in filling a class. Kate Williams Tabor '45 recalled a pleasant campus tour during her 10th reunion in 1955. She asked the student tour guide how many students were at Garrison Forest. After informing the group of the correct number, the tour guide paused, and then said, "Oh yes, and the 10 more Miss Offutt took." No beds were available on campus, but the headmistresses' community contacts and their charm ensured that these students were housed comfortably off-campus. Known as "out-boarders," handfuls of boarding students during the Marshall-Offutt era lived with local families. By the headmistresses' retirement in 1960, Garrison Forest's national reputation was considered highly competitive, and with a then-record enrollment of 296, the school had waiting lists for every class.

THE RULE OF LOVE

It is fitting, perhaps, that Miss Marshall and Miss Offutt, both formidable in spirit and unflagging in humor, would take the helm during such an uncertain financial time. Though they willingly acknowledged a lack of administrative experience and financial acumen prior to their arrival at Garrison Forest, their character and commitment to the students, faculty, and staff made up for their greenness.

Over the next 30 years, they would orchestrate Garrison Forest's emergence as a nationally recognized boarding school and serve as the architects for the school's modern era, creating rigorous, college-preparatory academics and exceptional riding and athletics programs and recruiting college-educated teachers from across the country. The campus additions they envisioned and championed still serve the school today: Shriver Hall, Senior House, Study Hall (now Livingston), the New or Big Gym (now the Old Gym), Robinswood, Meadowood, the riding complex, and the Chapel. Such achievements, though, might have seemed unlikely, indeed, given Miss Marshall and Miss Offutt's first year at GFS.

Initially, the women adopted very few rules, believing instead in the innate goodness of man and hoping that the girls would rely on their own consciences to make the right decision. "We didn't want rules," Miss Offutt wrote. "We felt we could rule by the rule of love…that people were always willing to learn." They believed that discipline, to be effective, "…must be recognized as having a purpose, that failure is never the end, that education in itself is an isosceles triangle—parents, children, teachers—and that no lack of understanding must be allowed to break the 'sides' of communication." Both were fond of the Socratic principle that "no one who knows the best can choose the less."

The few policies they did adopt were considered highly avant garde. First, they allowed the field hockey team to play without long, black stockings, which shocked their friends at the Bryn Mawr School and RPCS, Miss Marshall proudly recalled in 1956. Second, they allowed the seniors (with their parents' permission) and faculty to smoke on campus. The other two rules underscored the responsibility the women assumed for the students' safety and academic integrity: not leaving campus without permission and automatic suspension for the first cheating offense and expulsion for the second. Apparently, asking for permission to leave campus trumped informing the headmistresses with whom the student would be. In fall 1929, a mother arrived unannounced from Philadelphia to see her daughter. When she discovered that her daughter was not at school, the parent was told by Miss

The Chapel, a long-held dream of Miss Marshall's and Miss Offutt's, became a reality in 1959, a year before their retirement. Built with simple, yet elegant timber construction and soaring glass windows at the altar to frame the beauty of the woods, the Chapel's design captures the deep spirituality of the women that it honors. Used for weekly Vespers services until the mid-1980s, the Chapel is the location for non-denominational services, occasional alumnae weddings, memorial services for members of the GFS community, and the Junior/Senior Vespers each spring, where the "Light of Leadership" torch is officially passed from the departing seniors to the junior class.

Vespers were in the Little Gym before 1959.

Academic field trips and cultural outings have been part of the Garrison Forest curriculum since March 4, 1929, when teachers took the Upper School girls to Washington, D.C. to witness the inauguration of President Herbert Hoover. During the Marshall-Offutt era, the yearly school trip to Washington was a highly anticipated event worthy of front-page status in *The Blueprint*, the GFS student newspaper. Pictured on the U.S. Capitol steps are Miss Elizabeth White (top row, second from left) and some GFS students.

Offutt that the daughter was away for the weekend "staying with someone with a name like a fruit." The mother was not amused.

Though their philosophy that "fewest rules make for best government" was admirable, its implementation was less than successful. The need for more than just a few rules would become abundantly clear to Miss Marshall and Miss Offutt during their first year. Several students had gone to Washington, D.C. with permission to attend a performance at Ford's Theater. Miss Marshall received a phone call during intermission. The students were in a quandary. They wanted to smoke, but could not tell whether or not their consciences should allow it. Another unexpected phone call that first year came at 1:00 a.m. to Miss Offutt from the Pikesville police station in the early morning hours post-Maryland Hunt Cup, a spring steeplechase as well known for its tailgating as it is for its horse racing. Two students had been passengers in a car driven by boys, and the young men had gotten themselves into a fender-bender. After collecting the girls at the station, Miss Marshall and Miss Offutt shortly thereafter jettisoned their "ruling by love" doctrine.

THE SUM OF THEIR PARTS

Miss Marshall and Miss Offutt had been school chums at Bryn Mawr School. Miss Offutt graduated in 1915, and Miss Marshall had left school a few years earlier to travel in Europe before enrolling in the Sargent School in Boston to study physical education and graduating in 1916 with honors. Miss Offutt enrolled at Bryn Mawr College, where, in her own words, she "…spent two happy, thoughtless years, doing too little work, interested in too many things," before deciding not to return to college. While Miss Marshall served a stint in World War I as an Army nurse, stationed in San Antonio, Texas, Miss Offutt taught fourth grade at RPCS. After the war, Miss Marshall joined the RPCS staff as a coach and athletic director. Often they would discuss how they would run a school if given the chance. They "believed they understood children and…longed to put their theories into practice," wrote Miss Offutt.

Though they shared the same dream of leading their own school, their personalities, teaching, and leadership styles, and even physical attributes, could not have been more different. Straightforward and serious, robust and athletic, Jean Marshall's no-nonsense approach on the playing field and in the classroom was tempered with an infectious enthusiasm. Recalled Kitty Chaplin Martin '43, "She inspired us all to do better than we actually could, and we rose to the occasion." Miss Marshall the coach often chased her field hockey teams up and down the field if they did not run fast enough during practice. On weekend afternoons in the 1930s and early 1940s, she could be found recruiting boarders for a rousing game of football. Just as formidable on the basketball and tennis courts or on the back of a horse during a fox-hunt, she expected nothing less than a student's best, regardless of the girl's natural athletic abilities.

"Jean Marshall established quick rapport when we discovered that she could wield an expert hockey stick and shoot a fine basket," wrote Kay Dorr Sommers '33. "Nancy Offutt won our hearts just by being herself. Among all the women I've known since, she ranks highest in charm and gentle wit." Soft and round, with nary an athletic bone in her body, Miss Offutt's fey demeanor and whimsical approach made her a favorite of students, parents, and faculty alike, even if she was often late for class—or never showed at all—because of an appointment with her hairdresser. Her approach to life and administrative duties typically had a literary, reflective bent. "Everything was poetic in her life, whether she was writing poetry or writing a play for the Lower School…or whether she was thinking of

Miss Marshall coached field hockey for several years while serving as co-head-mistress and often ran up and down the field with her players during practice.

Miss Marshall, dressed here in her riding attire, also rode with students. Miss Offutt, however, preferred terra firma.

Tennis anyone?

Winter fun at GFS.

someone," said Kitty Marshall Washburne '46, Miss Marshall's niece. "She was wise about a great many things. If you wanted some real wisdom, you went and talked to Nancy. If you wanted some basic advice, you would go to Jean."

The women were quite different in the classroom as well. In addition to coaching, Miss Marshall taught ancient history, Bible, and History of Art, the latter a course that several alumnae cite as the most demanding of their education, at GFS and at college. Skilled at guiding students through challenging courses and athletic competitions, Miss Marshall's deep spirituality and love of the outdoors also left an impression. Alumnae recall her alto voice, full and resonant, singing "The Lord's Prayer" at Sunday evening Vespers as a member of the GFS Choir or leading hymns during morning Prayers. Her love of the outdoors inspired the same during spring walks with students through the Green Spring Valley.

Miss Offutt's teaching habits were decidedly looser, though her passion for classical literature and the English language equaled Miss Marshall's reverence for her favorite subjects. Kitty Hoffman '37 had been a student of Miss Offutt's at Bryn Mawr School before entering GFS in the eighth grade. "Miss Offutt would show up for a 9 o'clock class at 11," chuckled Kitty. "But she introduced us to classical literature. She read Shakespeare and the English poets to us, and gave me my real love of Shakespeare. We never had a bored moment in her class." In the earlier years at GFS, Miss Offutt taught English and performed all secretarial duties, the latter a task she laughingly characterized as a disaster. More often than not, the details of running a school escaped her mind. Sally Spilman Tufts '43 recalled passing a flustered and fast-walking Miss Offutt as Sally made her way to Manor House for lunch. "Oh dear," muttered Miss Offutt. "I forgot to order lunch today." The boarders had cheese and white bread that day, amid much laughter from everyone, including Miss Offutt.

Even their offices on the ground floor of Moncrieffe were a study in contrast. Miss Marshall chose the sunny Southwest corner and sunlight streamed through the chintz curtains, while Miss Offutt's office had dark paneling and dark leather chairs. Kitty Hoffman recalled once asking Miss Offutt why Miss Marshall had "all the nice decorations in her office." Miss Offutt smiled and replied, "Yes, but all the gentlemen come to my office."

Yet, for their differing demeanors, teaching styles, and even decorating preferences, they shared a quality that would help them form a seamless partnership. Headmaster Mr. Montgomery, who succeeded Miss Marshall and Miss Offutt, described the women's common personality trait simply as a "twinkle," a quality he defined as a mixture of humor,

mischievousness, naughtiness, and fun. The "Moffetts," as he
called them, "…didn't have any need to act like headmistresses of a
fine school because in the nicest and warmest way, they simply were
headmistresses of a fine school." He hastened to add that "neither were
innocents," particularly Miss Offutt. "She knew exactly the outcomes of her
most devious schemes, knew the right note to hit, and when to hit it…They
were not 'babes in the woods' easily deceived or misled. Further, they were
excellent judges of people. Garrison Forest was a place where the faculty
loved the kids, the kids loved the faculty, and the faculty loved each other.
All that wonderful stuff, mind you, because of the very special qualities of
those truly remarkable ladies who had run the show—not without error,
not without occasional serious miscalculations, not without some fairly
serious mistakes, but never without true humanity and the conviction that
all people, adults as well as children, deserve kindness and understanding.
They were really fine people with unlimited reserves of kindness and
warmth and humor."

This was not the case for teenage boys on campus after dusk. Rosalie
Brown Maury '35 wrote of "…some boys [who] crawled up a ladder to
Betty's [Elizabeth Williams Mustard '33] room; Miss Marshall spanked
them and sent them home." Such an obvious dismissal was not the case
when Miss Offutt attempted to let a faculty member go, as remembered
by Mary K. Boyd, chairman of the GFS French Department from 1938-77.
"Miss Offutt steeled herself for the ordeal, and gently, ever so gently,
[explained] to a smiling, nodding face. So gently, in fact, that one of the first
persons to appear in September was that teacher, who never grasped that
she had been fired."

Miss Marshall and Miss Offutt did not divvy up the many duties and
decisions of running a school. Rather, they met each challenge, decision,
and task with a simple, unwavering philosophy based on great mutual
respect for one another: They decided everything together, but whoever
felt more strongly would get her way. The school's motto was deeply
rooted in their approach to daily life at Garrison Forest and in their vision
of extending the school onto the national stage—and inculcating lessons
of authenticity within each student. "Miss Marshall and Miss Offutt spoke
the truth about everything—large and small," Sarah Whitaker Peters '42
remarked. "We, who were their students, do not forget it." The life lessons
imparted by the headmistresses had a tremendous impact on three decades
of Garrison girls. Said Carrington Dame Hooper '54, "We all learned from
[them] what 'ladies' were supposed to be. Their teachings went far beyond
the classroom and hockey field. They molded our spirits and confirmed that
we were special."

Sunbathing on the porch roof of the
Infantry.

Good times with friends.

Dressed for field hockey. The tunic
served as athletic team garb well into
the 1970s.

Eating lunch on the front lawn of Manor House.

Miss Marshall behind the wheel of her car with Miss Offutt in the back seat.

Jenny Burton Parr, also a 1954 graduate, recalled a story that embodies Miss Offutt's innate kindness: "There was a girl in our class who for some time had been the butt of our jokes. To our surprise, Miss Offutt seemed to know all about it, and we were summoned to her office. We received a lecture, but her final remark I have never forgotten. She said to us, 'It is so easy to be mean, but it takes great imagination to be kind.' She was a lady of infinite wisdom. We were properly admonished but also challenged." These lessons and the headmistresses' personal examples offered a stark contrast to the images and national ideal of subservient female perfection that were being communicated in the media and the culture. Dickie Buck Miller '54 noted that her "...avid feminism for the rights of women has its genesis with Miss Marshall and Miss Offutt, two superb role models who encouraged women to seek higher aspirations, an idea that was generally lacking in the blandness of the 1950s."

On a pleasant spring morning in the 1950s, Miss Offutt's car, Puddles, decided to make a break for it, a mechanical feat made easier when Miss Offutt absent-mindedly failed to engage the hand brake. Miss Offutt looked out her classroom window and saw Puddles heading toward Reisterstown Road. She calmly turned to her students and beckoned them to the window. "Come look at Puddles running away to that awful road," she said. Just when disaster seemed imminent, Puddles took a sharp left, aided by a bump. The car's new course led it across the lawn and hockey field and into the tennis courts where it stopped at the net. Miss Offutt then excused the class so the students could go congratulate Puddles for wanting to go home to Evenlode, the headmistresses' nearby residence. Another Puddles adventure involved Miss Offutt coming to a senior English class without the students' papers. She blithely explained to the perhaps-not-surprised class that she had placed all the graded papers on Puddles' rear bumper while running errands in Pikesville and had driven off, scattering the papers along Reisterstown Road. Miss Brown [Elizabeth Brown, head resident and head of the athletic department] combed the bushes along the road and recovered some, and it is alleged that the state police returned a few others.

RIGOR AND WARMTH

The headmistresses and their faculty and staff guided, encouraged, and sometimes cajoled students into achieving more academically, athletically, artistically, and personally than perhaps the girls thought possible. Though "the emphasis has always been on teaching and those intangibles that are called spiritual values," wrote Miss Offutt of the school's educational philosophy that continues to this day, having students go on to enroll in college has been part of the school's tradition since its founding. The first two GFS graduates in 1914 were accepted into Bryn Mawr College. Yet, from 1928-35, no GFS student emerged as a candidate for admission to a major college. This was less a fact, perhaps, of the curriculum and quality of the students and more a reality of the drop in GFS enrollment numbers during the earliest years of the Great Depression. Kay Dorr Sommers, one of seven members of the Class of 1933, was the only senior preparing for college.

By spring 1935, a student was, once again, accepted by Vassar. "We were in the Big League, at last," wrote Miss Offutt. By 1955, approximately 90 percent of all upperclassmen were enrolled in the college preparatory track. That year, only two seniors had what was called "Special Senior" status, meaning they had completed 15 credits toward graduation. Though no diploma was conferred for the Special Seniors, they enjoyed such senior privileges as residing in Senior House and processing with their class at graduation. If a student could not or did not intend to receive a diploma, the headmistresses did not encourage students to remain at GFS after sophomore year, but to select another school with less rigid graduation requirements. Girls, however, often ignored the advice and remained at Garrison Forest.

Miss Marshall.

Sledding on campus.

GARRISON FOREST AND WORLD WAR II

On Sunday, December 7, 1941, the news of the Japanese attack on Pearl Harbor spread among the GFS students and faculty. Some students, still dressed for riding, gathered around a radio at the Green Spring Valley Hunt Club with club members to hear President Franklin D. Roosevelt tell of "the day that will live in infamy." Others recall seeing the December 8, 1941, *Baltimore Sun* on the Manor House steps and hearing the frightened breakfast conversations that ensued.

Reading *The Blueprint*.

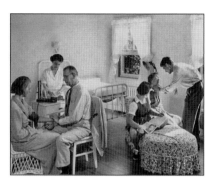

Dr. Palmer F. Williams, school physician from 1930-74, tended to the health of the school community in the Shriver Infirmary. His family continued its GFS association with his son Dr. McRae Williams joining his father as GFS physician from 1969-73. Daughter-in-law Ruth Williams taught math at GFS, and granddaughter Ruth "Puddin" Williams graduated in 1987.

Named for George M. Shriver, the school's longest-tenured President of the Board, Shriver Hall was built in 1939 as a dormitory and infirmary, with a science laboratory in the basement. The Class of 1939 gave the wrought-iron railing with the school crest.

Much changed on campus after that fateful day. Though no Victory Garden was planted on campus and gas rationing kept students from participating in U.S.O. or Red Cross activities as an organized school group, GFS did its part on the home front. Courses in home nursing and first aid were added to the curriculum, taught by student Kitty Chaplin Martin '43, a trained Red Cross volunteer. Students learned aircraft identification and practiced blackouts. A few refugees from war-torn England found their way to GFS, including Georgina Dobrée '46, and art teacher Christine Nisbet and Sylvie, her young daughter. With the campus staff diminished, students took on the responsibility of cleaning their own rooms, waiting tables in the Dining Hall, using dinner knives to cut onion grass out of the Manor House lawn, and helping with the tack in the stables—the genesis of the work program, a GFS tradition that continues to this day with students assigned to help clean up classrooms. "The school was very much aware of the course of the war," wrote Miss Offutt. "Mutual anxieties, interests shared, and the need to find their own amusements at school, drew faculty and students together in close association. In retrospect, the war years were for many of us a period of purpose as well as waiting."

Just as they had done during the previous war, students took to nearby fields to help the school's neighbors harvest apples or harvest corn. Service League, Garrison Forest's umbrella organization for community service, was founded by the students in 1942, and during the war years, students focused their service efforts on the home front. In addition to helping local farmers, the girls sold war bonds and stamps and filled Christmas stockings for soldiers. Miss Marshall and Miss Offutt regularly invited a speaker to Prayers to explain what was happening on the front lines in Africa, Europe, and the South Pacific. During Study Hall, books were closed for 15 minutes to allow students to gather around the radio and listen to Edward C. Murrow's *This is the News*. With weekend trips into Pikesville and downtown somewhat curtailed with gas rationing, faculty helped students find on-campus fun. Miss Boyd used war rations for occasional weekend French cooking lessons, making rationing seem chic by teaching the girls to make vichyssoise.

War rations challenged the school's talented kitchen staff. Courtney Garland Iglehart '48 remembers many a school lunch and dinner of just asparagus on toast, and Miss Offutt was not above using her wit and charm to ensure that her girls had enough butter, sugar, and other carefully rationed foods. During the war, she received a phone call from the rations board to attend a hearing. The school had used up its rations coupons, and Miss Offutt had requested more. As Pemmy France Noble '48 recalled, a day or two before the meeting, Miss Offutt conveniently "contracted" a contagious disease, and then promptly called the rations board to let them know she was coming and alerted them to the state of her health. "They, of course, in horror said, 'Don't come,'" said Pemmy. Miss Offutt's response was, "Then you will give us those extra coupons." When the rations officials explained that they could not do that, Miss Offutt insisted that she would come immediately, "sick" or not. They begged her to remain on campus, to which she sweetly replied, "Then you will give us the coupons?" They did. "She was persuasive," laughed Pemmy.

The war also altered Commencement plans and inspired a little penny-pinching patriotism. The U.S. government had asked that civilians limit their travel, thus spring vacations during 1943 and 1944 were cancelled. Classes continued during what would have been a two-week break, and graduation was pushed up two weeks earlier. The Garrison Forest graduation dress tradition continued throughout the war, however. Until the 1970s, students from fifth grade up were required to wear white dresses and attend Commencement. During wartime, students had to make do with clothing they had or hand-me-downs. Recalled French Shriver Foster '42, "You saved your white dress and passed it down to a classmate the next year. People could not afford to buy a new one."

Art class, 1947.

During the Marshall-Offutt era, it was a school tradition for all students, even the coed Infantry, to dress in white and process by class at Commencement.

In 1936, the school purchased Senior House, the white clapboard house near Moncrieffe, as a dormitory. The traditional home to the senior resident students, the building also serves as the background for the class photo taken just prior to processing across campus for Commencement.

A NATIONAL PRESENCE

Working in the science laboratory.

With enrollment growth, more faculty, and an expanding campus came another important milestone: incorporation as a not-for-profit in 1938. With this designation, the school also officially claimed what had been its unofficial name since its founding. No longer The Green Spring Valley School, Inc. on paper, the school legally became Garrison Forest School, Inc. The stock certificates issued in 1912, the time of the purchase of the current property, were exchanged for income bonds due in 1958.

Several stockholders, including Board President George Shriver, immediately contributed their stock to the school, thereby writing off thousands of dollars of obligation by Garrison Forest. The trustees voted in May 1954 to offer to purchase any remaining bonds (at the time, $67,000 total), four years earlier than noted in the 1938 incorporation. Every bed filled and the school's debt was paid. With a burgeoning GFS endowment (first established in 1944) providing scholarships, a faculty pension program, and helping to close the gap between yearly available income and the institution's needs, Garrison Forest had achieved financial solvency by 1954.

Leaving Study Hall with Miss Brown (in light coat at the top of the steps).

Growing the small, country school into a national presence took more than fiscal planning, though. It required vision, determination, a healthy dose of luck, and good timing. During one of the earliest pre-accreditation visits by the Maryland State Department of Education, Miss Offutt created her own luck. The GFS faculty and headmistresses had decided that, no matter what, the state official was not to witness fourth period math, which one faculty member dubbed "unresponsive." Miss Offutt, acting as tour guide, forgot the edict and promptly ushered the official to the math class. She left the visitor in the room and blithely went off down the hall. Miss Brown met her and admonished her for leaving him in the one place he was not supposed to be. "Never mind! I fix!" was Miss Offutt's reply. She pulled the fire alarm, and the math class was the first to exit the building. She casually mentioned to the official as they stood on the lawn watching roll call that she thought he might want to see a fire drill. As students shuffled back into classrooms, she led him to a French class.

Greeting new girls at Manor House.

The New Gym or Big Gym was built in 1942 and was truly multipurpose as the venue for athletic contests, assemblies, performances, Commencement, and some chapel services (prior to the 1959 construction of the Chapel). Once a year, it even doubled as a final exam locale, with Miss Marshall covering nearly every surface with posters of artwork for her comprehensive History of Art exam. Armed with bluebooks and (hopefully) knowledge, students had to pace the gym and name and describe as many artworks on posters as they could. When the Elizabeth B. Searle '74 Athletic Center was added to the campus in 2002, the older gymnasium became known as the Old Gym and home to the Lower Division's gymnastics equipment.

Graduation, circa 1950s, in the Gym. Note the art posters on the walls from Miss Marshall's History of Art final exam.

Suzanne White Whitman, director of riding from 1930-60, played a key role in boosting the school's reputation beyond Maryland. It was perhaps fate and not luck that compelled her in September 1929 to ride her horse onto campus from her nearby home. As Miss Marshall's cousin, Mrs. Whitman was well acquainted with the new leadership of Garrison Forest. She listened to Miss Marshall and Miss Offutt lament the fact that there were few students. Mrs. Whitman enthusiastically offered her services and vast network of contacts on the equestrian and tennis circuits to boost regional recruitment. "Let me get into the racket—I'll start riding and fox hunting, [and] we'll compete with Foxcroft," she wrote.

Mrs. Whitman threw her considerable charm and connections behind creating a nationally known boarding department, and as head of riding, developing a top-notch riding program. During its earliest days, GFS attracted its share of boarders, typically from the Baltimore region and the nearby Mid-Atlantic states, though in 1929, one of the boarders hailed from Illinois. "One day I said to the heads: 'A-hunting we must go! We took the sleeper to Pittsburgh where my sister…had invited over 50 mothers to meet us for tea…We turned on our charm and traveled home with six girls in our bag." By 1935, students were coming to board at GFS from as far afield as Hawaii, Minnesota, and even Chile. It was not just Mrs. Whitman who convinced many parents. "Jean and Nancy charmed every parent," wrote Mrs. Whitman. "One of [my friends] said to me, 'It's a dump…and I can't resist those two women.' "

According to Mr. Montgomery, the trio of women formed an "unspoken stratagem and became a formidable team in the exercise thereof." In layman's terms, they created what he dubbed the most artful admissions scam this side of Las Vegas. First, Mrs. Whitman told her friends far and wide that Garrison Forest was highly desirable and fiercely competitive, and that, of course, she would be happy to put in a good word. During a visit to the school, parents would be told that GFS would be delighted to have the child come, but the best they could offer at that point was a place on the waiting list. Parents and applicants were encouraged not to give up hope, and upon returning home, in a few days, an acceptance letter would arrive, followed in the next day's mail with a contract. "The real message is that Jean and Nancy and their team did a superb job with those girls both personally and academically once enrolled," he noted. Apocryphal or not, the admissions program he described worked. By the time Mr. Montgomery took over the reins in 1960, Garrison Forest was one of the most competitive girls' boarding schools in the country, with bona fide waiting lists for every class.

Mr. Montgomery laughingly recalled how Miss Offutt's poor admissions record-keeping helped to create a strong class. What he called a "cherished bit of the school's mystique" involved a ninth grade child (and a GFS legacy) who was deposited with luggage on the Manor House porch on an opening day of school in the 1950s. Her parents were nowhere to be found, nor was any admission or rejection letter. "Nancy knew all about the child," Mr. Montgomery said. "She and Jean had decided that with greater vigor in the academic program, it would not be in the child's best interests to admit her. Under considerable pressure to do something, Jean and Nancy decided that they surely must have sent the wrong form letter. They had no choice other than to make a place for this child." Four years later on the night before the student's graduation, Miss Marshall and Miss Offutt decided that they would tell the parents, whom they assumed knew nothing of the school's comedy of errors, which had worked out for the best after all. The parents looked at each other, smiled, and admitted that there had been a rejection letter, but that they knew if they sent their daughter anyway, Garrison Forest would take care of her. They were right.

Enjoying a campus visit by the Good Humor Man.

Study Hall, 1955.

Riding to the hounds.

Miss Marshall's History of Art class was as inspirational as it was rigorous. Students painstakingly compiled illustrated notebooks to complement their textbook. Miss Marshall's two-volume course outline set the standard for the level of mastery she expected from her students.

The Meadows with a few of Miss Offutt's favorite animals grazing on the lawn.

Miss Marshall and Miss Offutt sit for their portrait by Maryland-born and Gilman-educated artist Trafford Klots (1913-76), son of portrait painter Alfred Partridge Klots and Agnes Boon Klots. The setting they chose for their portrait was the Chapel. The painting hangs in the lobby of the Upper School academic building that bears their name.

THE MEADOWS

In 1948, the trustees purchased Evenlode from Miss Marshall and Miss Offutt. This white, clapboard house originally sat along Reisterstown Road near the entrance to the school. In the 1930s, the women had purchased Evenlode as their own home and though it was situated just off school grounds, it was certainly part of the campus. Boarding students were invited there on weekends to share a cigarette with Miss Marshall, and faculty dinners and trustee receptions were held at Evenlode.

Miss Marshall and Miss Offutt, though, dreamed of owning a farm. Both had grown up on farms—Miss Marshall in Roslyn and Miss Offutt in Towson—and both loved animals. Sheep, in particular, were a favorite of Miss Offutt's. According to several alumnae, when someone would point out to Miss Offutt the sheep's reputation for not being the brightest in the barn, Miss Offutt would reply, "Yes, but they are so Biblical."

In 1948, they bought an 18th-century plantation and dilapidated stone house and barns known as the Meadows, overlooking the Red Run Valley in Owings Mills. Less than three miles from campus, the Meadows had more than enough space for the women, their dogs, and school events, including the end-of-year faculty party and graduation activities. Mrs. Nisbett, the art teacher for one year during World War II, and her young daughter lived at the Meadows. Students would often visit on Saturday afternoons and help with such farm chores as shucking corn, burning underbrush, and painting chicken houses.

Miss Marshall and Miss Offutt restored the house, as much as possible, to its original Colonial roots by removing bay windows and a third-floor addition, which Miss Offutt said gave the home "the appearance of a rundown summer hotel"—exactly what it was on occasion. During his GFS interview in 1959, Mr. Montgomery and his wife Anita stayed at the Meadows. In the morning, the headmistresses announced that the plumbing had "gone south," he recalled. "Not one bit perturbed, Jean and Nancy set out with Anita in tow for the north fork of their freshly flowing creek, and I was given explicit instructions for the proper use of the south fork. Thank the Lord that we remembered to [pack] bathrobes. Had we forgotten, it would have made no difference…to those extraordinary ladies. Matters that superficial meant nothing to them."

The school commemorated the headmistress' retirement in June 1960 with numerous dinners and festivities and gifts from the alumnae: a silver tray and an all-expenses paid trip to the headmistresses' beloved Greece and Italy. The Alumnae Association had collected $3,600, an effort that the alumnae managed to keep secret until the gift was presented. In her thank-you note to Alumnae Association President Louise McKinney Warner '36, Miss Marshall expressed her delight: "What can Nancy and I say to all you dear children of ours? When the heart is full, words become few. I can only tell you that we both are deeply touched by your loyalty and love…As for a trip abroad, a real trip for more than six weeks, is something of which we could only dream— now it can be a reality…" During their April 1961 trip, Miss Offutt wrote an open letter to the alumnae with details of their itinerary and the sights they enjoyed. She ends it simply: "It is our sorrow that we cannot thank you, each one. You have given us more than you can ever know."

After retirement, the headmistresses remained active on the GFS board, reviewing applications for admissions, and enjoying close relationships with the succeeding heads and the alumnae who had been their students. (A trip to the Meadows was de rigueur when alumnae visited Garrison Forest.) Both women remained at their beloved Meadows until their deaths (Miss Marshall died on September 24, 1973, and Miss Offutt on March 1, 1982).

Their legacy and the impact of their fortitude and vision changed Garrison Forest forever from the small, country school founded by their predecessor, Mary Moncrieffe Livingston. "Miss Marshall and Miss Offutt could not have possibly surmised at that time what the future had in store for their newly acquired family, but they set about with joyous determination to make a go of it," wrote Latin teacher Miriam Vanderveer in 1960 to mark the school's 50th anniversary. "With all the changes and growth, the

Miss Marshall and Miss Offutt, pictured here in 1937 enjoying one of Italy's modes of transportation, loved to travel abroad.

Miss Offutt and Miss Marshall laying the cornerstone of Meadowood. The building was named as the result of a contest; the winning entry prompted the dry-witted science teacher Kathleen Gran to note that perhaps Senior House should be renamed as "Seniorswood" and "Seniorswouldn't." In addition to housing student dormitory rooms and faculty residences, Meadowood has been home to the library.

cornerstone of Meadowood laid by Miss Marshall and Miss Offutt remains— faith in the individual, joy in working with her and willingness to give always and completely to her…We shall try to keep the qualities of simplicity, graciousness, and courage which Miss Marshall and Miss Offutt have given us—qualities that have kept Garrison Forest from becoming ostentatious, pretentious, and complacent."

HOORAY FOR HOLLYWOOD!

An undated mea culpa from John Barrymore to Miss Marshall and Miss Offutt following his first visit to campus.

Actor John Barrymore and daughter Diana Barrymore '40 during one of his visits to Baltimore.

When Miss Marshall and Miss Offutt entertained visitors, they used gold-rimmed plates monogrammed with the school crest.

During the 1930s and '40s, two of Hollywood's leading men, John Barrymore and Henry Fonda, were occasional visitors to Garrison Forest. Diana Barrymore '40 was the daughter of John Barrymore of the famed Barrymore acting dynasty and poet Blanche Oelrichs, who tried from afar to script her ex-husband's visits to GFS. The rule was that Mr. Barrymore could visit, but Diana was not to leave campus with him. His first visit with tea and dinner in Manor House passed without a hiccup. After showering Diana with gifts from his travels, he left for the Belvedere Hotel in downtown Baltimore.

His visit the following day strayed far from the script. Miss Marshall and Miss Offutt agreed to his request to treat Diana and a friend to dinner off campus. Paparazzi swarmed the table and snapped photos of the actor and his daughter, and afterward, Mr. Barrymore treated Diana and her friend to a movie and a nightcap. At 1:00 a.m., the taxi pulled up to Manor House. Miss Marshall was waiting on the porch. She sent the girls to their room, poured two cups of hot coffee into Mr. Barrymore, and sent him on his way. The story goes that before departing in a taxi, he leaned over and kissed Miss Marshall on the forehead. During a subsequent visit, he took several day scholars and boarders out to dinner with the promise to return them to campus by 10 p.m. An hour after curfew and with no sign of the dinner party, the headmistresses called the day students' parents to explain why their daughters would be late. The parents were so delighted that their daughters were at dinner with Mr. Barrymore that it mattered not what time they arrived home.

Henry Fonda's occasional visits to stepdaughter, Frances "Pan" Brokaw Corrias '49, were far more staid. (Her mother, Frances Seymour Brokaw Fonda, was Mr. Fonda's second wife and the mother of actors Jane and Peter Fonda.) His quiet, reserved on-screen persona was reflected in his infrequent visits to campus, sometimes with his wife, son Peter, and young daughter Jane in tow. Pan's classmate Sally Gardner Willis recalled having lunch with Sally's mother, fellow senior Anna Hanes Chatham, and the Fondas at the Green Spring Valley Hunt Club. "Mr. Fonda was very quiet and didn't say much," recalled Sally. "Jane Fonda never said a word. She sat there with the biggest blue eyes and a big blue bow in her hair."

Henry Fonda's stepdaughter, Pan Brokaw Corrias '49.

For nearly 20 years, the Infantry was home to Garrison Forest's youngest students, for whom Miss Offutt wrote annual plays.

THE INFANTRY

Under the watchful eye of Rhoda Archer Penrose—"Mrs. Penny" to her enraptured young charges—from 1930-48 the Primary Department continued Garrison Forest School's founding commitment to the education of preschool-aged girls and boys. Children as young as four and five enrolled in the Infantry, and boys typically attended for two years, while most girls continued at Garrison Forest. The Primary Department (nursery through grade four) was housed in the Infantry, a converted stable with classrooms and hayloft-turned-art and music studio. Presiding over the children was Mrs. Penny—tiny, prim, and upright, with snow-white hair. She demanded discipline and manners from her young ladies and gentlemen, but was always ready to lend a sympathetic ear or to dry tears. She instilled a love of beauty in her students by reading poetry at rest time and directing the children in tableaus and plays written by Miss Offutt.

Mrs. Penny's mission was not just fanciful fun. She provided an early, indelible introduction to the arts and a classical education with her presentations of Della Robbia friezes, stained glass, and relief sculpture reproductions. Under her precise direction, costumed students would re-enact scenes from her art collection by standing silent and ram-rod straight on the cubbies in front of an audience of parents and other teachers. "At Christmas, we did a tableau of Pompeii," said George Shriver III, who attended the Infantry from 1938-40. "Two of us [held] a stretcher with two dead ducks that a parent had just shot. I remember the smell."

Mrs. Penny's appreciation for beauty, pungent or otherwise, was not limited to the arts. She planted and maintained an expansive garden at the Infantry, convincing students that fairies lived there. Kitty Marshall Washburne '46 recalled walks around the campus with Mrs. Penny. "One day she took us out on the porch in the snow and asked us what we saw that wasn't there before," Kitty remembered. "The answer was tiny bird footprints." Each spring, Mrs. Penny sponsored a wildflower contest, open to any student in the primary grades. The rules were simple: Collect and correctly identify the most wildflowers and the winner would get his or her name engraved on the Wild Flower Cup, which was presented at the GFS graduation. Competition could be fierce and dynasties were not unheard of, recalled Ally Lou Hackney Altstatt '45, who enrolled at GFS as a second grader: "I was always beaten out by the Fisher family, which had seven girls and one boy. Finally the Fishers grew too old for the Infantry and I finally won my fourth year." When Ally Lou started in the GFS Lower School, she trained little brother Hap, a GFS first grader, for the Cup. "I would send him to school each morning in the springtime, clutching a wilted bunch of wildflowers and a list I had him memorize. Lo and behold, he won the Cup that year—the first boy to win it!"

The Infantry was originally the school's stable until its 1930 conversion into primary classrooms and living quarters for Mrs. Rhoda Penrose, head of the Infantry.

Music classes were an important part of the Infantry's program.

Pictured here is Mrs. Penrose, "Mrs. Penny" to the students, in her Infantry garden.

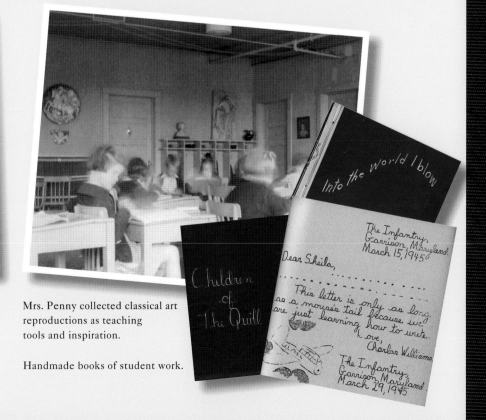

Mrs. Penny collected classical art reproductions as teaching tools and inspiration.

Handmade books of student work.

GROWING A FACULTY

When asked what the reasons were for the school's success, Miss Marshall and Miss Offutt placed the faculty at the top of the list. "If we had not found the right kind of teachers, we should not have attracted the children, who, second, have made and are making Garrison hard-to-get-into," Miss Offutt remarked in a 1955 interview. In 1929, they inherited a strong faculty of nine women, including Margretta Whiting (art), Roberta Glanville (music), and history teacher Dorothy Hall. Many of the school's founding and early faculty members hailed from the Baltimore and Mid-Atlantic region. Miss Marshall and Miss Offutt cast their net wider to fill faculty vacancies and to create the teaching staff they envisioned to take Garrison Forest's reputation nationally. Though their strategy was sound, their interviews with national candidates were a bit unconventional. In 1944, Miss Offutt hired a young Nancy Parker, a Briarcliff Junior College graduate who taught riding at a camp in Colorado, to be a riding instructor. The interview consisted of a campus tour with little conversation other than Miss Offutt pointing out various buildings and classrooms. At the end of the tour, Miss Offutt turned to the young woman and asked coyly, "You like?" Miss Parker replied, "I like." "You come?" "I come," was the young woman's answer. For the next six years until her marriage, Miss Parker taught riding, tutored Latin, attended to office duties, and directed school plays, including "The Road," Miss Offutt's original, beloved Christmas play, a job Miss Parker (later Mrs. Welbourn) continued as a Garrison Forest parent well into the 1970s.

Miss Brown, an early hire by Miss Marshall and Miss Offutt, with students.

DOROTHY HALL

Hired by Miss Livingston in 1919, history teacher Dorothy Hall also ran the Infirmary and the fledgling riding program prior to being tapped by Miss Marshall and Miss Offutt as assistant headmistress in 1929, a position Miss Hall held until she retired in 1960. Miss Hall's quick wit and wisdom and enthusiasm for all things Garrison Forest served her well as head of Senior House and as a trustee—and served the school immeasurably.

Miss Brown's "contract" to join the GFS faculty:

ELIZABETH BROWN

From 1938 until her retirement in 1970, Elizabeth Brown's duties were many at the school: head resident; athletic department chairman; hockey, basketball, and tennis coach. If anyone had a question, Miss Brown—the students called her "General Brown"—had the answer. She handled travel arrangements, special events, permission slips for weekends away, rooming assignments, mealtime seating arrangements, scheduling for all athletic teams, and student banking. With her ever-present ruler, she was in charge of measuring the length of students' skirts and issuing demerits should a hem be deemed too short. Her purview extended to the philosophical as well, with Miss Brown instructing New Girls how to behave and counseling seniors as they prepared to leave Garrison Forest. Her bookkeeping acumen tallied all Light Blue and Dark Blue points. Fittingly, the annual spirit award given at Commencement to the most spirited class in each division bears her name. Miss Brown, who died in 1992, was named an honorary trustee in 1977.

February 22, 1938
Dear Elizabeth:

Nancy and I are perfectly delighted to know that you have crossed the Rubicon and decided to come along with us at G.F.S.

I hope you won't be disappointed and that something really worth while will be forthcoming for all of us. If the war doesn't break out, or we all become paupers, I see no reason why in the next few years we shouldn't be able to make salaries which will make it possible to save appreciably for our old age—cheery thought.

We never have had contracts but keep this letter as our agreement—that we promise to pay you $1200 posthence and $1300 if there should be anything in the woodpile.
Sincerely and gratefully,
Jean

Miss Simpson.

Miss Simpson (left) and
Miss Porter (right).

BARBARA PORTER AND ELIZABETH SIMPSON

In fall 1944, recent Bryn Mawr School graduate Barbara "Babs" Porter was working as a file clerk in a Baltimore pharmaceutical company when her mother received a phone call from her friend Jean Marshall. Garrison Forest was in need of a math teacher, and the job was Miss Porter's if she wanted it. "I told [Mother] I didn't know a thing about teaching," Miss Porter chuckled. "She told Miss Marshall that she would have to call the Bryn Mawr headmistress and get [a recommendation], since I had not done well at school except for math." The next day, Miss Marshall called the Porter household asking if Miss Porter could start on Monday. And she did, though she was barely older than her students. "It wasn't easy to teach [the students] as far as discipline because I was really just about their age," she recalled. For 42 years, she taught fifth through twelfth grade math. In the 1960s, she served as the part-time Director of Admission, and was later Registrar for a year following the death of Elizabeth "Betty" Simpson in June 1985. During the 1970s and '80s, Miss Porter, an accomplished pilot, taught a popular (and difficult) aeronautics elective, Ground School, during which she instilled her love of aviation in GFS students.

Miss Simpson was hired a year after Miss Porter, also to teach math. She shared her friend's keen analytical mind and penchant for precision. Well-spoken and outspoken, the Vassar-educated Miss Simpson was an advocate for faculty and a favorite among students. During the 1970s, headmaster Larry Hlavacek tapped her for the duties of Registrar, which she ably handled while teaching upper-level math courses—two roles she continued until her death.

Mrs. Vanderveer in her Latin classroom.

Faculty, 1950.

MIRIAM VANDERVEER

Known simply as "Mrs. Van," Miriam Vanderveer was one of the first hires the young headmistresses made. A Bryn Mawr College graduate with a degree in Italian, Mrs. Van was hired in August 1930 to teach English. When she arrived at her new job, Miss Marshall and Miss Offutt informed her that, due to the unexpected departure of the Latin teacher, Mrs. Van would be filling that vacancy. During her first year at GFS, Mrs. Van, who had studied Latin, stayed a few chapters ahead of her students. She also learned to teach standing up—a lifelong habit inspired by a student placing a thumbtack on the teacher's chair. A master Latin teacher and effective administrator, Mrs. Van chaired the Latin Department and served as college counselor during her 42-year tenure. As a Quaker, she often took groups of students to local Quaker Meeting for Worship gatherings. As secretary to the GFS board from 1960-74 and a trustee Emerita thereafter, she rarely missed a board meeting. She was doggedly persistent about the need to raise teachers' salaries and provide for their retirement—two issues often overlooked for the typically all-female, often single teachers who filled the positions at all-girls schools until the 1960s. A generous donor to GFS throughout her life, Mrs. Van's $4.2 million bequest following her death in 2001 to support faculty salary endowment remains the school's largest, one-time gift to date.

MARGARET HERBERT, R.N.

Margaret Herbert nursed many a young GFS patient back to health. Her hiring, though, was somewhat unorthodox. In 1956, Garrison Forest was without a nurse. Trudy Harris Harder Burton, mother of Jenny Burton Parr '54, had worked with Miss Herbert at New York City's St. Anne's Maternity Hospital. St. Anne's wanted Miss Herbert, then 65, to retire, but she wanted to continue to work. It took only one phone call to Miss Marshall to solve both parties' occupational dilemmas. Jenny's mother called Miss Marshall and told her that she found her nurse. "Miss Marshall asked if she knew how to nurse, and Mother replied 'yes.' I don't think Miss Herbert ever interviewed," Jenny recalled of Miss Herbert, who stayed at GFS until her retirement in 1969.

KATHLEEN GRAN

The formidable Kathleen Gran led students through an exacting education in biology, chemistry, and physical science during her GFS tenure from 1940 to 1971. With a sharp intellect, a proud Yankee heritage from Wareham, Massachusetts, and a wry sense of humor (and "quite the twinkle in her eye when she got a notion to share it," remembers friend and fellow science teacher Winifred McDowell), Miss Gran was demanding of herself and expected the same from her students. For her, instilling critical thinking skills was as important as providing a solid science education. If a student yawned in class, the austere Miss Gran promptly sent her outside for oxygen, recalled Ally Lou Hackney Altstatt '45. "She was strict but she didn't seem to get mad when we'd drop test tubes," chuckled Ally Lou. A campus resident for 31 years, Miss Gran was head resident of Shriver for many years and rarely missed any extra-curricular event on campus. If an opinion was needed, hers was the one that was sought. After her retirement as chairman of the science department, the GFS Board made her an honorary trustee, a position she enthusiastically and seriously undertook until her death in 1994.

ROBERTA GLANVILLE

Roberta Glanville (pictured below right) led the music program and choir with keen musicianship and a steady hand. As passionate about singing as she was about athletics, Miss Marshall also lent her rich alto voice to the GFS Choir, singing beside her students at school and community events, including St. Thomas' services.

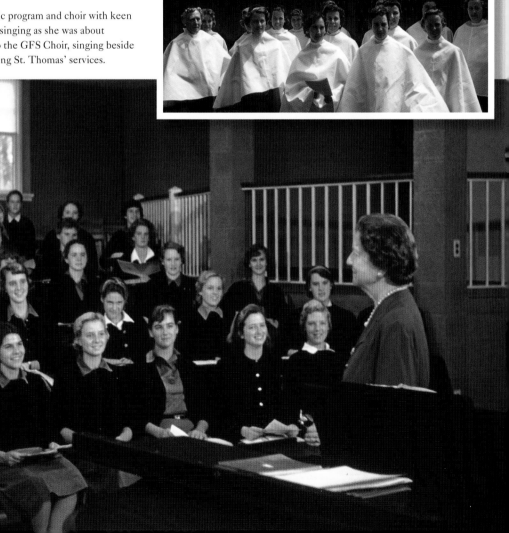

Preparing for the faculty basketball game, 1940s.

MARY K. BOYD

Mary K. Boyd began her 40-year Garrison Forest career in 1937 as chairman of the French Department and retired in 1977 as the same and with the added title of honorary trustee. A devoted Francophile and consummate scholar—she penned several articles in French for *The Blueprint*—Miss Boyd also coached badminton, was head resident of Moncrieffe, resident of Senior House, and advised French Club. Of her own accord, she led Prayers once a week throughout her GFS years. Her reason was practical—she wanted to give the heads the "morning off" for personal errands—but the impact on the students was far more philosophical, thanks to her reflective readings, often from Kahlil Gibran's *The Prophet*. Though a proud daughter of Columbia, South Carolina, Miss Boyd's French was impeccable, honed by a year spent as a Fulbright scholar in France before accepting the GFS job (much to her Southern mother's chagrin). She was a demanding teacher, particularly regarding pronunciation. Shocked at how little students in the 1950s knew or cared about world events, she instituted a weekly current events quiz to raise awareness and discussed the events of the day (in French, of course) with her class. She had respect for her students, addressing each student in her class as *Mademoiselle*, and often sharing her impish sense of humor. Her precision was just as evident outside of class. She insisted that all food be eaten with utensils, and no one sat down to dinner unless each student had turned off the lights in her room. Miss Boyd faithfully checked each dorm room before dinner and sent any offenders back to turn off the lights.

Miss Boyd.

Leaving the Infantry., 1967.

ARCHIBALD R. MONTGOMERY III
HEADMASTER, 1960-1968

"Have you seen him?"

"What's he like?"

(The Blueprint, March, 1960*)*

The students were abuzz as they filed into Study Hall for Prayers on the morning of March 14, 1960. Questions circled around the room until 8:50 a.m. when the recently appointed Garrison Forest School headmaster stepped into the room. All chatter stopped, as Archibald "Tad" R. Montgomery III introduced himself to the Lower and Upper School students. For the next three weeks, he attended classes, and spoke to students, faculty, and parents as part of his orientation for the role he would assume on July 1, 1960.

Two years earlier, when Miss Marshall and Miss Offutt announced their intended retirement in June 1960, the board turned to its network of parents and alumnae to recommend candidates. Mr. Montgomery was among the first to be nominated, and in his initial thoughts, an unlikely choice to lead a girls' school. At the time, he was teaching English, serving as admissions director, and coaching football, baseball, and ice hockey at his alma mater, the Westminster School in Simsbury, Connecticut. "Not exactly what one was expected to do at a girls' school," he chuckled. "I was as much a coach as a teacher, but my Garrison Forest friends thought that I would like [Garrison] and that the school would like me." Still thinking that it was "very, very unlikely" that he would lead a girls' school, he agreed to an interview. "In order to be polite, we thought we needed to go, but we [told] them we were predisposed not to do this," he said. He and wife Anita visited the campus and, as Mrs. Montgomery recalled it, they simply fell in love with Garrison Forest.

The feeling was mutual. Mr. Montgomery, the unanimous choice by the board's Selection Committee (its members included Miss Marshall and Miss Offutt), became the first headmaster of Garrison Forest. Handsome, charming, and easy-going described not just Mr. Montgomery, but his

The Trustees
of the Garrison Forest School
are happy to announce
the appointment of
Archibald R. Montgomery, III
as Headmaster
to succeed
Miss Jean Gilmor Marshall
and
Miss Nancy Jenkins Offutt
Headmistresses

July 1, 1960

The Montgomery family photographed at GFS (left to right): Tad holding Katie, Anita, Eliza, Anita holding Carolyn, and Arch.

Mr. Montgomery lends a hand on campus.

elegant wife Anita and their children Archie, Anita, and Eliza. (Katie and Caroline joined the Montgomery clan during the family's GFS years. To celebrate the occasions, their father cancelled classes on the days of their births.) Born and raised in Philadelphia, Mr. Montgomery was a former Marine who served two years in the Pacific during World War II. He received both his undergraduate and graduate degrees from the University of Pennsylvania.

The young couple—Mr. Montgomery was 36 and Mrs. Montgomery 26 when they came to GFS—made quite an impression on campus. "We were enchanted by them," remarked Melissa McCarty Warlow '62. "This was a Kennedy-eqsue family—glamorous, articulate, with Kennedy-esque children." Mrs. Montgomery agreed, citing the phrase used to describe the country's presidential administration at the time: "It was Camelot."

During his three-week visit in March 1960, and throughout his first year, Mr. Montgomery quickly dispelled any concerns that, after such a long and charmed chapter in the school's history, he would usher in changes and alter Garrison Forest's character. He praised the "rare simplicity of Garrison Forest," noting that it was precisely this quality that had charmed him and his wife. "Many schools strive for years for such a spirit of unity and happiness," he wrote. "On it depends success or failure, and at Garrison Forest…it comes so naturally."

Mrs. Montgomery with a group at Lochinvar.

MI CASA, SU CASA

The Montgomerys opened up their home to the campus community as never before. "Girls seemed to live at our house," recalled Archibald "Arch" R. Montgomery IV, or "Archie" to the GFS girls. "They were always coming and going." Mrs. Montgomery redecorated Evenlode with "everything geared for practicality" for a growing family—and a few hundred surrogate daughters. On Saturday nights, boarding seniors entertained their beaus in the living room with Mrs. Montgomery in the house, but not in sight except to deliver soda and cookies. Every other Sunday evening was reserved for senior boarders (the other boarding classes took turns during the off-weeks) to come and talk after Vespers about issues concerning school life. Topics ranged from the students' desire for more social activities to adding more bread choices in the Dining Hall. Mr. Montgomery also assigned all senior day and boarding scholars to small discussion groups to meet with him regarding morals, student/faculty football games, and everything in between.

Students came to Evenlode for cider in the fall, hot cocoa in the winter, and Easter egg dyeing in the spring. Then there was the boarders' mad dash down to Evenlode after Wednesday night study hall to smoke as many cigarettes as they possibly could in 45 minutes before heading back to the dormitories. When students knocked on the door in search of a shoulder to cry on, Mrs. Montgomery was there. "She was a gem," recalled Brigid Devereux Kernan '65. "I was a very homesick new girl, and she comforted me and listened while I cried." Margo Chisholm '66 added: "She was available to have conversations that I could never have with my own Mom, wonderful as she was. Anita made me feel important, heard, of value in a way that I don't think I understood until years later."

The feeling of family was reciprocated. Numerous students babysat the headmaster's growing brood and fetched the telephone-books-cum-booster-seats for the children to use in the Dining Hall during dinner. Riding Club members taught the Montgomery children to ride, and Mr. and Mrs. Montgomery also rode with the students. Mr. Montgomery often was found guarding the faculty goal during the annual faculty/student hockey games or playing lively games of softball and tennis with the students. An invitation to the Montgomerys' home, Dining Hall table, or even a walk down to the hockey field was a treat. "We respected them both and wanted to be in their company as much as possible," wrote Betsy Bishop Nolan '66. "They shepherded us through laughter and tears, blizzards, and fine spring days when we could not or would not pay

The sign announcing the headmaster's home also meant "All Students Welcome Nearly Anytime."

Having fun in front of Robinswood.

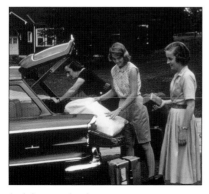

Arriving at school.

Thanks to their easy rapport and close relationship with the students, very little escaped the Montgomerys' watchful eyes. "I remember senior spring when Chuck [a boyfriend] drove down from Middlebury several weekends in a row and was around campus as much as he was allowed," said Margo Chisholm. "Then one Wednesday morning Mr. Montgomery and I were leaving breakfast...and there in the circular driveway was a little white Austin Healey with a very male elbow hanging out the driver's side window. Mr. Montgomery looked at me and said, 'Isn't that Chuck?' My first thought was, 'How does he know that? Oh God, has Chuck been around that much?' Then my face turned bright red as I answered in the affirmative. The Montgomerys were kind enough to let Chuck hang out in their house while I was in class and to let me visit with him a bit in the afternoon which, as I recall, was definitely 'outside the rules.'"

attention, growing up, good sportsmanship, relationships that became life-long friendships, math, biology, lacrosse, and *Annie Get Your Gun*."

The former headmistresses also were frequent guests and great counsel to the young headmaster, and apparently to his son. "Miss Marshall and Miss Offutt named their hamster after me," recalled Arch Montgomery. "I was honored, as you can imagine." They also pitched in with family chores, occasionally driving Arch to and from Gilman School where he was enrolled. (Decades later, Arch Montgomery would serve as Gilman's headmaster from 1992-2001). Miss Marshall and Miss Offutt—or the "Moffetts" as Mr. Montgomery good-naturedly called them—were a tremendous help to Mr. Montgomery. "Institutions take on their own character, and they understood this," he said. Miss Marshall and Miss Offutt continued to attend GFS athletic matches, plays, and concerts, and to provide a historical perspective or a sympathetic ear. "Every once in a while, when we had to dump a kid out of school or do something that was unpleasant, they would invite [Anita and me] over to the Meadows for a couple of good solid drinks and dinner...They seemed to know when you were bleeding a little bit."

Built in 1937, Study Hall was a main academic building for the Upper School until 1974 when Marshall-Offutt opened. When The Valley School merged with Garrison Forest in 1975, Study Hall became home to the primary grades, and in 1995, the building was expanded and renovated to accommodate the kindergarten through fifth grade program. Now called Livingston, the building's architectural and ornamental elements served as inspiration for the expansion. The relief sculpture on the wall of Study Hall is a copy of the ancient Greek Amazon Frieze. It was acquired in 1937 by Miss Marshall and Miss Offutt from their alma mater Bryn Mawr School. It continues to hang in its original spot.

HIGH EXPECTATIONS

Mr. Montgomery was immediately struck by the school's commitment to each student. "When it took a child, Garrison Forest did everything in its power to see that the child was successful," he said. "What that really meant was that there were two tracks, the college preparatory track and the general program. I don't believe that the girls felt divided, because there was a very real quality of scholarship across the curriculum." In his first few months as headmaster, he lost no time in introducing new, mostly academic, programs, with the changes "…designed to emphasize the raison d'etre of Garrison Forest School: attention to individuals." With the trustees' approval, in January 1961, he implemented an eight-week seminar in literature for GFS seniors who were Honors students, which he himself taught in his office.

Other curricular changes included the addition of one hour of daily physical activity, Oriental studies, and modern dance, the latter a month-long course taught in January by a Bennington College student. The school's traditional Bible class, a weekly, required, no-credit course, was amended to present the Bible as literature within the English curriculum. Mr. Montgomery also instituted a popular artist-in-residence program, bringing a writer or visual artist to campus for several weeks.

The Class of 1968's *Ragged Robin* letter to the headmaster expressed the students' appreciation for the Montgomerys' attention: "Any girls entering Mr. Montgomery's office are greeted with, 'Hello, kids, what can I do for you?' This is Mr. Montgomery's entire approach, one of optimism, encouragement, and genuine concern. Whether it be a pat on the back and a 'How's it going?' or a snowball fight, his interest means a great deal to us."

His ability to listen with a patient ear and kind heart also thwarted a would-be runaway student during Mr. Montgomery's first year at Garrison Forest. Jill Irvine Crow '61 had made up her mind to run away from school. "I was having a difficult time in my life and had planned to leave," said Jill, who confessed to her roommate her plans of hitchhiking on a horse van to get to her brother in California. The roommate, in turn, alerted Mr. Montgomery, who immediately called Jill into his office. He spent hours with me, and at the end of the conversation, just said, 'Stay.'" The next day—the day of Jill's planned departure—Mr. Montgomery was attending his sister's wedding. Before he left campus, he implored Jill to stay, at least for the weekend, until he returned. At Vespers that Sunday evening, Mr. Montgomery saw her and winked. She had decided to stay. "I credit him

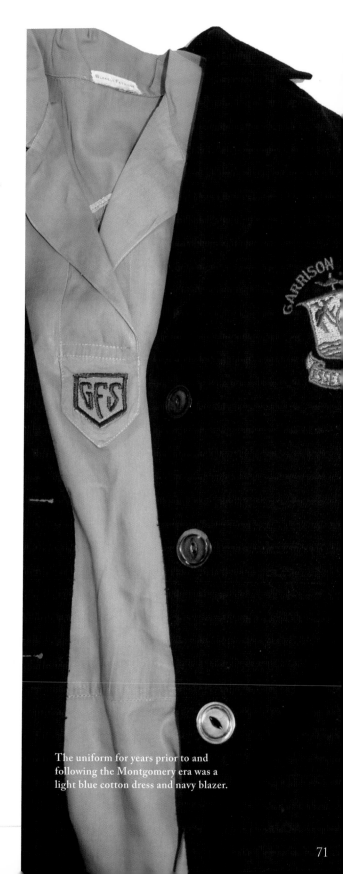

The uniform for years prior to and following the Montgomery era was a light blue cotton dress and navy blazer.

A kind friend to the students, Alfred West drove the GFS bus for 39 years.

A much-anticipated part of the school day: getting mail.

with totally saving my life," she said. "He was a very fair player, and I thought the world of him."

On weekends, day scholars enjoyed dates, parties, movies, and shopping on Baltimore's Howard Street, and other off-campus activities. Boarders would be invited to join them, often using their allotted two weekends and one night away from campus for an overnight with a day scholar. However, if one lived on campus, having fun outside of class and clubs required a little creativity. Every Saturday afternoon at 2 p.m., Alfred West, the school's bus driver from 1939-78, picked up boarders on a first-come, first-served basis for the weekly trip into Pikesville. The route for the boarders was well established: first to Fields Pharmacy for a crab cake or something else from the soda counter, followed by a visit to the make-up counter. Then it was on to Vince's Pizza, with a final stop at the five-and-dime store before catching the GFS bus at 3:30.

"We created a lot of our fun," remembered Stuart Rinehart Stewart '66, who, as a freshman, bought guppies in Pikesville to raise in the dorm. As sophomores, she and classmate Mimi Haentjens Stone purchased stamps in Pikesville to re-sell for a profit back at school until they were shut down by the no-nonsense campus resident and Lower School physical education teacher Nan Taylor. When it snowed, the girls went sledding in front of Manor House on trays from the Dining Hall.

A highly anticipated daily event for the boarders was dinner, not so much for the food, but for what would follow after Miss Brown rang the hand bell she kept near her seat. The first bell indicated that it was time for grace and announcements, of which the latter included singing congratulations to anyone with exciting news, mainly a college acceptance or invitation to attend a dance weekend at a boys' school. Parents—and more importantly, boys—knew to call the Manor House hall telephone during dinner. "Blakely Fetridge Bundy '62 remembers the electricity in the room when Miss Brown would ring her big bell and announce, "Telephone call for…" "The so-anointed student would bound out to the hall phone to take her call, hoping against hope that it would be a boy," she recalled. "When she returned to the dining room, everyone would ask who had called. Most likely it was her parents, which she would report with an indifferent shrug. However, if it was a boyfriend, she'd report so with a big smile on her face."

Warmer weather heralded another favorite activity: sunbathing. Again, the rules of engagement were very well-defined. First, Miss Brown and Miss Taylor had to deem the weather suitable. If the climate cooperated, the women would raise the designated "Sunbathing Allowed" flag at Manor House. There were guidelines as to the exact locations where students could sunbathe: Meadowood porch and on the back lawn of Senior House only. Cardboard sun reflectors were forbidden. If students were found using them, the contraband would be confiscated and the owners required to claim them in front of the school during Prayers. And one was certainly not allowed to meander about campus in a swimsuit or towel. Even with such exacting rules, Stuart Stewart recalled a few seniors managing to embrace *Esse Quam Videri*'s implicit celebration of authenticity by pushing the sunbathing restrictions to eliminate as few tan lines as possible. Later generations followed suit.

Dramatic productions are a long-held tradition at GFS, beginning with plays performed under Miss Livingston's direction by the earliest students to entice new families to enroll. Miss Offutt directed and wrote numerous plays throughout her tenure, and students performed the classics as well. Pictured here is a play with McDonogh School (above) and a production in the Little Gym, circa 1960s.

	IX	X	XI	XII
ENGLISH	Study of American literature. Composition and Grammar.	Study of English literature, Beowulf to Johnson. Composition.	Study of English literature. Johnson to present time. Outside reading and Composition.	Study of world literature. Composition. General review for college preparatory students.
HISTORY	Ancient	Medieval (Elective)	Modern (Elective) U. S. History	U. S. History
MATHEMATICS	Algebra through Quadratics.	Plane Geometry	Intermediate Algebra and Completion of 3 Math. Units (Elective)	Solid Geometry and Trigonometry (Elective)
SCIENCE		General Science (Elective)	Chemistry Biology	Chemistry Biology
FRENCH	Study of basic principles of Grammar. Vocabulary building and verb forms. Reading of standard texts.	Careful study of fundamentals of Grammar. Stress on application in written work. Reading from standard authors.	Summary review of Grammar. Extensive reading from standard and contemporary authors. Special emphasis on French oral reports and recitations. (Elective)	Survey of French Literature (Elective)
LATIN	Fundamentals of verbal constructions.	Caesar	Cicero (Elective)	Virgil (Elective)
HISTORY OF ART				Comprehensive Survey of Art. (Elective)
SPANISH			Study of elementary vocabulary and grammar, training in understanding, speaking, reading and writing simple Spanish. (Elective)	Study of fundamentals of grammar. Vocabulary building. Reading from standard texts. Oral and written work equally stressed. (Elective)
			Social and political geography of the world.	Comprehensive Survey Comparative Religi

The Ins, a student-created folk-singing group.

A skit in 1964.

Tea after a field hockey game.

CHANGING TIMES

The Montgomerys' youth and charisma mirrored that of the White House in the early 1960s, and such qualities were perfectly suited to help usher in the cultural changes emerging in the nation. During his eight years at the school, Mr. Montgomery hired younger faculty members and a few married dorm residents to provide younger role models to the students and to further the feeling of "family" on campus. In his first year, he made a radical decision and hired the type of faculty member never before seen in a GFS classroom: a man. "I was the only trousers in sight," joked Mr. Montgomery about his arrival on campus. There were a few men on campus working in the stables, kitchen, and on the physical plant staff, but none on the teaching faculty.

For one year, professional portrait painter Samuel Gholson taught art history in the Upper School. In fall 1964, Richard Watts, Ph.D., joined the faculty, teaching English, Government, and music appreciation. *The Blueprint* announced his arrival with the headline: "Panic! Man on Campus!" For nine years, Dr. Watts regaled students with his travel tales from Russia (he spoke the language fluently) and instilled in his English students a love of literature and a questionable appreciation for memorization. (He required that his Honors English students memorize 1,000 lines of T.S. Eliot's *The Wasteland*.) Dr. Watts also handled the part-time college counseling duties—a full-time position for college counseling would not be added until the mid-1980s. In 1961, J. Sawyer Wilson III became the full-time Business Manager and taught a mathematics review course to the students. Mr. Montgomery's other barrier-breaking early hires included Donald Elliott, Sr. as librarian.

Of course, women were still the majority on the GFS faculty in the 1960s and remain so today. Mr. Montgomery's leadership in recruiting and retaining male teachers went hand-in-hand with his strategic efforts to improve faculty compensation and benefits for all GFS teachers. Increasing faculty salaries, which were "not at the level of the good New England schools…and not even [approaching] the salaries offered in the public school system," was frequently discussed at trustee meetings. Less than a decade earlier, the board had established a faculty pension, and in 1961, approved $8,000 to help address salary discrepancies, a figure that would rise during Mr. Montgomery's tenure to more than $20,000 annually for salary increases.

During an October 1965 board meeting, while discussing the turnover of young, single female teachers, Mr. Montgomery quipped that "…able young women tend to marry." Attracting a married, male teacher to the staff and providing him and his family with non-dormitory living quarters was critical, he felt. The school had recently purchased Kohler Cottage for just such a family, which became the home for math teacher Peter Whiting, his wife, and their three children. In 1966, Donald Elliott, Jr. succeeded his father as GFS librarian, joining the English department faculty as well. He, his wife Cielito Elliott, and their five children moved into Evenlode, which had been vacated by the Montgomerys when they moved into Lochinvar, the recently purchased "castle" overlooking the campus. (This move did not keep the elder and enterprising Montgomery daughters, Anita and Liza, from picking apples from the trees surrounding Evenlode and trying to sell them back to the Elliotts.) Mrs. Elliott, a Peabody-trained concert pianist, joined the music department, teaching generations of young GFS pianists until her retirement in 1999. In 1971-72, Mr. Elliott made a permanent move to the classroom to teach humanities until his retirement in 1996.

Just as the GFS classroom was beginning to change with the addition of male teachers and new courses, so too was the business of independent schools. When Mr. Montgomery arrived at Garrison Forest, many independent schools had already sought and received accreditation from the appropriate state or regional accrediting governing bodies. Garrison Forest had chosen not to seek accreditation during the latter part of the Marshall-Offutt era. Accreditation became another popular trustee topic in the early 1960s. The GFS board determined that "the value of accreditation lies in enabling the school to escape from state supervision…," regarding the number of school days and teacher certification. Thus, on November 11, 1966, a 16-member evaluation committee from the Middle Atlantic States Association of Colleges and Secondary Schools visited campus for three days. Garrison Forest received the highest rating (five) given by the accreditation board, with the evaluation committee complimenting the "fine school, enthusiastic and loyal student body, the dedicated faculty." The only areas for citation were a lack of facilities for math and science, and the need for increased library and auditorium space.

Donald Elliott, Jr. and wife Cielito "Cely" Elliott set the bar high at GFS for intellectual curiosity and artistic expression.

A Peabody-trained pianist, Mrs. Elliott joined the music department in 1966, and during the course of her 33 years on the faculty—nine of those years as department chair—she taught hundreds of GFS students and other budding pianists from around the region. Her connections with many classical musicians infused the music department with talented teachers and artists, bringing flutist Clinton Arrowood, choral director Theodore Morrison, pianist Reynaldo Reyes, and others into the department.

A talented athlete, Mr. Montgomery often played goalie in faculty-student games.

"Ours was either the first or second Senior Dance Weekend to be held and it was a huge deal! There were weeks of preparation, and the excitement mounted day by day. There was always much talk about boys and boyfriends, but these boys were rarely seen. In fact, many had grown into mythical giants through months of description and discussion. Suddenly these romantic, handsome 'gods' were going to be on campus in the flesh. Suddenly, everyone's descriptions got more realistic, knowing that these boyfriends would be eyed and evaluated by all. We'd hear disclaimers such as 'He's really not that attractive,' or 'He's kind of short.' Realism set in. All the boys hung out with Mr. Montgomery and thought that he was a great guy, probably a bit younger and more relaxed than the traditional headmaster at the New England boys' schools. What a change for us 1962'ers, who spent our childhoods in the 1950s but, by the end of our college years, were thrown into the freedom and chaos of the 1960s."
—Blakely Fetridge Bundy '62

WHERE THE BOYS ARE

For all the fun that the members of the boarding community were creating on their own, there was one essential piece missing: boys. Several boarders had beaus who would visit Evenlode, and later, Lochinvar, to call on their dates, but the students wanted more. During the Montgomerys' first year of student gatherings, they heard about the need for social events. During the last decade or so of the Marshall-Offutt era, there were neither on-campus dances nor any school-sanctioned activities that involved boys. "The girls were dying to have a good, up-close look at a boy," said Mr. Montgomery, "so we said we would invite them to our campus and have a dance."

In 1962, after much planning on the part of the Montgomerys and several faculty members, Garrison Forest hosted its first dance. One way or another, every student had a date. During his tenure, these one-evening-only events evolved into an annual dance weekend with activities for girls and their dates from Friday through Sunday brunch, a distinction among girls' boarding schools. "We were one of the first boarding schools to have weekends with boys," Mr. Montgomery recalled. "It was important for the kids to be a little worldlier before they went off to college." Dates stayed in Moncrieffe, chaperoned by Mr. Montgomery, while the Moncrieffe boarders bunked with other girls in Senior House and Shriver.

The Montgomerys also arranged bus trips for GFS students to attend football games and dances at Woodberry Forest, St. Andrew's, the U.S. Naval Academy, Episcopal, and other regional boys' schools. Typically, dates were waiting as the GFS bus pulled up, randomly assigned by height. The school also arranged for joint Glee Club concerts on the Garrison campus with St. James and McDonogh singing groups and their GFS counterparts. Sometimes students suggested dance destinations. In 1967, Andy Vaughan Detterline '68 convinced the Montgomerys to arrange Garrison Forest's first dance at The Hill School in Andy's hometown of Pottstown, PA. "Hill did not have any dances with a school as far away as GFS, so they neglected to ask us for dinner," she chuckled. "My mother invited the girls and chaperones to our home for dinner prior to the dance. We arrived (about 100 strong) in three charter buses." Mrs. Vaughan set up food stations throughout the ground floor of the house, even recruiting Andy's older, college-aged brothers to return home to serve the girls. She neglected, however, to consider what havoc 100 high school girls might wreak on the house's 5 1/2 baths. Despite the well running dry, the dinner and dance were great successes, Andy recalled, especially for her mother: "Mr. Montgomery ended up at Hill as headmaster the next year, and he hired my mother as the alumni director."

The closer proximity to the opposite sex may have inspired the students' request for education on sex, drugs, and alcohol. With the support of the Board of Trustees, in October 1967, Mr. Montgomery formed the Steering Committee for a Human Relations Program to cover these issues. "…Because of the constant publicity given to the problems of alcohol, drugs, and sex and the inevitable discussion of them…," Mr. Montgomery hoped to provide the students with factual knowledge and "a sense of values" needed to face these issues. The committee, of which Mrs. Montgomery was a member, created faculty-led small discussion groups for students to answer any questions on the subject.

Mass marketing of the sexual revolution was in full swing by 1967. Seven years earlier, the Federal Drug Administration approved the birth control pill. In 1961, Helen Gurley Brown challenged traditional sexual mores in her best-seller, *Sex and the Single Girl*, and in 1962, Betty Friedan stirred up gender roles in *The Feminine Mystique*. By the 1960s, the majority of American homes had a television set, as did the GFS dormitories, allowing students to watch the revolution unfold on screen. A few issues on campus with sex, drugs, or alcohol were beginning to creep in during the early- and mid-1960s, but the school maintained careful oversight of such matters. Quipped Mr. Montgomery, "We kept a pretty good eye when a couple would disappear [from a dance]."

Showing off the school banners.

Getting ready for the big dance with big curlers.

The tradition of dance cards continued through the Montgomery era. Girls would "fill" the card with boys' names by talking with their friends prior to the dance and always reserving the first and last dance for their date. Dances were often held in the Manor House dining hall (pictured left) or in one of the gyms.

Enjoying a well-chaperoned evening on campus.

"The day President Kennedy was shot, I was driving home from school with Alfred [West] on the school bus. I was the first girl to get on and the last to get off, living…downtown in Bolton Hill. Alfred and I spent a total of three hours together every day for my five years at GFS. We talked about everything. We were pals. That day, the President was still alive, and the radio was playing nothing but very minimal reports of his condition and endless opinions and observations of the event, mostly repeating what little was already known or thought. The bus emptied out. I was then alone with Alfred, both of us focused on the radio. I kept saying, 'Don't worry, Alfred, they can save him.' A few minutes before my stop, they announced the President's death. Alfred flipped off the radio, and we drove the rest of the way in silence. There was nothing either of us could say."

—Sally Adamson Taylor '66

DEFINING ISSUES

The revolutionary aspect of the 1960s went far beyond sexual mores and manners. Change was coming quickly to the world beyond Garrison Forest. On Friday, November 22, 1963, the school day was just ending when word spread across campus that President John F. Kennedy had been shot during a Dallas motorcade (12:30 p.m. Central Time). Most day scholars already had left campus—classes were over by 12:30 p.m. on Fridays—and boarders were scattering to afternoon activities. Anne Smart Pagano '69 had just finished working off her demerits by polishing shoes. While walking back to the Lower School, she ran into a classmate who told her that Kennedy had been shot. "We played a lot of practical jokes on each other quite often, so I did not believe her," said Anne. "I laughed and challenged the story. I soon realized that she was really serious, and with that…came a sensation like being kicked in the stomach."

Day student Francie Gorman '67 was walking past Manor House on her way to play rehearsal when suddenly another student ran out and said that the President had been shot. Francie joined a group of girls crowded around the television set, "…not exactly sure what was happening, but unable to tear themselves away." She recalled that the student in charge of play rehearsal insisted that the girls adjourn to the Old Gym, which they did reluctantly. In the middle of rehearsal, around 2:00, a few girls who had been listening to a transistor radio announced the breaking news: "He's dead." Rehearsal

stopped as students stood in shock, some crying. Mrs. Montgomery, who first heard the news on the car radio as she was pulling into her driveway, quickly joined the students in the Gym. "Mrs. Montgomery kept us all calm. There was always a solid, calm strength about her that I so respected, admired, and counted on," said Margo Chisholm '66, who was among the students in the Old Gym. Shortly thereafter, Mr. Montgomery assembled in the Gym any students, faculty, and staff remaining on campus to discuss the day's events and to grieve as a community. Days later, students gathered around the television console in Meadowood would witness the live broadcast of Jack Ruby shooting Lee Harvey Oswald.

Garrison Forest was arguably sheltered from many of the events embroiling the nation during the early 1960s, but issues were discussed. Mrs. Montgomery recalled that student gatherings at their home often led to serious discussions about civil rights: "We were young enough to be caught up in an active way, and we did a lot of talking in those days."

Sometimes the reality off campus smacked against the reality on campus. Andy Detterline remembered her birthday party in the basement of Senior House the week of Reverend Dr. Martin Luther King's assassination, which occurred on April 4, 1968, and was followed by rioting in cities across the country, including Baltimore and Washington, D.C. "We didn't realize that there were riots going on at the time," she wrote. Her party coincided with one of the first warm days of spring, so the girls opened the sliding doors. "We were having a sock hop to blaring music. The police came because they thought the noise was some sort of civil rights uprising. They joined us for cake and then went back to work—a pretty surreal event for all concerned."

The board's steps toward integrating Garrison Forest began in 1961 with the adoption of an open admissions policy. In the November 1966 *Blueprint* article "PROBLEM: INTEGRATION," a student reported on an Upper School discussion about integration. Citing the school's five-year-old open admissions policy that "any girl who is fully qualified and who can meet the admissions competition will be accepted regardless of race, color or creed," she reported that only three African-American girls applied for 1966-67, though none enrolled. "Baltimore was a very Southern city when we arrived…and there was a flavor of prejudice," Mr. Montgomery noted

The school's first African-American students Greta McDonald Anderson '74 and Shelia Love '74 (Shelia, above right) unintentionally inspired a uniform change that remains today. After a year or so of the girls walking up the long Manor House driveway from the bus stop during winter, Greta's mother petitioned headmaster Lawrence L. Hlavacek (1968-78) to allow to them to wear pants to school—and to keep them on during the school day. "My mother never came to campus because she was a little intimidated," Greta said. "But this was the one time she went to speak to Mr. Hlavacek." He agreed, and after Greta and Shelia started wearing pants, other students quickly followed suit. Thus, after seven decades of a skirt or dress-only uniform policy, the uniform included blue pants.

in an interview 40 years later. The anonymous comments from the school community quoted in the 1966 *Blueprint* article underscore this. One person questioned whether "…a certain number of parents would withdraw their children…" Another expressed the need "…to ask for volunteers…for students to room with an African-American boarder." Mr. Montgomery said he was not aware of any teachers' feelings, pro or con, on integration, but noted, "They knew exactly where I stood on the matter." *The Blueprint* article, though, ended on a hopeful note: "The student body, I believe, would welcome a Negro student. In the life of tomorrow for which we are preparing, it is essential that we be without prejudice. True tolerance is built on experience, not idealism."

At the following February trustee meeting, Mr. Montgomery announced three "negro applicants for the Lower School in 1967." This time, two girls chose to enroll: Greta McDonald Anderson and Shelia Love, both of whom graduated in the Class of 1974. To recruit the school's first students of color, Mr. Montgomery worked with the now-defunct Training Now for Tomorrow (TNT) program run by Marise Ross, an enterprising, white, suburban Baltimore housewife, who, in 1963, "adopted" a group of high-achieving African-American students attending a Baltimore City public junior high school. She solicited funds from friends, foundations, and companies to take the students on cultural outings and educational trips. As described in a *Life* magazine article about TNT, her initial goal was to "…get [them] interested in college and mold them into richer material in the competition for college scholarships." Her program quickly evolved into a scholarship program to place her students into Baltimore's independent and parochial schools.

Shelia was the first to come to Mrs. Ross's attention. "Mrs. Ross was on a mission to send me to Garrison Forest School," said Shelia, who lived with Greta and her family as their foster daughter. Both girls attended Windsor Mill Elementary School, a public school in West Baltimore, and because of the living arrangements, Greta's parents decided that Greta would attend GFS as well. "I was terrified that first day," Greta recalled. She had "never been in the minority before," and was nervous about the differences between her old school and the new one: "It was my first year of French, and I had never changed classes before or taken books home. I didn't feel accepted initially because I felt too overwhelmed…but I had teachers [at GFS] who were extremely warm and protective."

Getting to school required rising at 6:00 each morning to catch two Maryland Transit Authority buses for the hour-long, one-way commute. In many ways, their commute was emblematic of their role in breaking the color-barrier at Garrison Forest and the impact it had on both their school and home communities. Initially, Greta was terrified of riding the bus. "I had never been on a public bus in my life," she recalled. "My father was a science professor at Morgan State University and my mother taught English [at the secondary level]. I was very sheltered, but Shelia wasn't." During their first year at GFS, Greta and Shelia began changing out of uniform before they left the Lower School. "We got harassed enough [on the bus] for having books," noted Greta. "Having books and a uniform was too much." She recalled bus drivers having snacks for them and throwing off the bus the children who harassed them.

"We lived in two very different worlds," Shelia reflected. "I remember feeling like I was there to get an education, and that kept me grounded." That dichotomy was never more evident than during their commute in early April 1968. Neighborhoods in East and West Baltimore, and across the country, were rioting following Dr. King's assassination. Shelia recalled waiting for the bus in West Baltimore, with only city buses, police cars, and National Guard vehicles on the streets. When they arrived at Garrison Forest, what they were witnessing at home, several miles from campus, was not discussed, said Shelia: "The riots and Dr. King's assassination were not talked about."

Greta was co-president of the ninth grade class and part of Service League, and Shelia was Light Captain in the Lower School (and in eighth grade was cast as Mary in "The Road" Christmas pageant), but between bus schedules and homework, they did not participate in many school activities. Missing the bus meant waiting an hour for another bus, though Greta laughingly recalled that they were not averse to walking one mile south on Reisterstown Road to the next bus zone to save 10 cents, which meant they both could enjoy a Little Tavern hamburger before going home. When the girls transferred buses at Slade Avenue in Pikesville, the older African-American women who were regulars at that stop fretted like doting grandmothers over the girls. "They would sit with us between them to keep warm…and tell us how proud they were of us," Greta recalled. Garrison Forest's African-American kitchen staff also felt the same sense of pride: "[They] loved us and gave us anything we wanted to eat."

Ironically, Greta credited Garrison Forest for introducing her to black history and literature, which had not been part of her public elementary school's curriculum. The GFS assemblies in 1968 included an African jazz ensemble, and a year later, the Upper School offered a non-credit, minor elective course, Black Literature. "Race, poverty, and urban life and culture were topics of conversation, especially in Mr. Elliott's class," she recalled. It was his Minority Report elective that introduced her to what

An influential and much-adored figure who eased Greta and Shelia's transition into Garrison Forest was Frances Elizabeth "Betty" White, Lower School head from 1941-70. She oversaw grades five through eight with a kind, calm presence and a leadership style that modeled competence and constant compassion. Greta recalled mentioning to Miss White that she felt slightly uncomfortable in a class. The next day, Miss White attended the class, standing quietly in the back, her kind yet no-nonsense demeanor sending a clear message. "She was very gentle and never yelled," Greta said. "I always thought of her as a marshmallow, so soft and fragile, with her matching sweater sets and sturdy shoes." Miss White's daily habit of reading aloud to students after lunch created indelible, warm memories and a love of literature in generations of girls. The F.E. White Building, named for Miss White, opened in 1974 and housed the Middle School students and teachers until 2007, when the new Middle School building was constructed.

Miss White gave each eighth grader in 1950 a wooden spoon inscribed with "Best of luck to my spoon-fed Eights."

Pictured here are students circa 1960s streaming from Moncrieffe, the first new building to be constructed on the Reisterstown Road campus. Moncrieffe symbolized the growth and future of Garrison Forest. Originally a four-story stone and timber structure, the 1920 building housed student and faculty dormitory rooms, classrooms, and offices. Donors had hoped to name the new building for Miss Livingston, a request she declined but compromised by allowing the building to have her middle name. It ceased to be a dormitory in the 1960s, but remained a vital classroom facility. Since the 1980 renovation, Moncrieffe has been home to the preschool division.

became favorite books: Zora Neale Hurston's *Their Eyes Were Watching God* and Chaim Potok's *The Chosen*. "Mr. Elliott understood discrimination [from] being part of an interracial couple," reflected Greta on his marriage to Cely Elliott, who was Filipino. "I always felt that he 'got' me…As difficult as it was, I really enjoyed my time there."

Greta and Shelia remained the only African-American students at the school during their three years in the Lower School. When they entered the Upper School, a few other African-American students enrolled. Garrison Forest's tight finances in the 1970s did not allow school-funded transportation for students, and for students needing scholarship money, Garrison Forest-funded scholarships and outside funding were scarce. During the 1980s and '90s, racial and cultural diversity increased dramatically, influenced by such factors as the Green Spring Valley and its surrounding area becoming more multicultural, and international boarding increasing significantly in the early 1990s. By the end of the first decade of the 21st century, students of color represented 25 percent of the school's student body.

Most importantly, the trustees and subsequent heads of school embraced Mr. Montgomery's vision of what Garrison Forest School could and should be. Shelia harkened back to another GFS leader, founder Mary Moncrieffe Livingston, to sum up her experience: "With Garrison Forest and its motto, *Esse Quam Videri*, you truly learned to develop character. Learning to respect people's differences is part of that."

Joining GFS in 1966, first as librarian and then as a full-time member of the English faculty, Don Elliott, a natural at the Socratic method, posed endless questions to his eager students. With patience and an unwavering respect for the ability of the teenaged mind, he would answer questions with more questions. A graduate of the Great Books program at St. John's College and a self-taught classical pianist, Mr. Elliott shared his voracious love of literature and music on campus. The salons hosted by the Elliotts in their Evenlode living room were popular with students and colleagues. Mr. Elliott, who retired in 1996 and died in 2001, also was the Morning Meeting accompanist and an avid participant in faculty/student softball and football games. In 2001, several alumnae established the Donald S. Elliott Faculty Sabbatical fund, which is granted annually to a faculty member who exhibits Mr. Elliott's Renaissance qualities. The first recipient was Kim Marlor, GFS tennis and badminton coach since 1986, physical education chair, residential faculty for 17 years, and avid lifelong learner, who spent her sabbatical in Peru on a GFS trip.

Aerial view of campus.

A DEVELOPING CONCERN

By the early 1960s, the genteel horse and buggies and clanging streetcars on Reisterstown Road were long gone. "That awful road," as Miss Offutt called it, was now a bustling, four-lane thoroughfare increasingly lined with commercial, industrial, and residential development. Interstate 695 (the Baltimore Beltway) was completed in 1962, and a northwest expressway (I-795) to link Owings Mills, Reisterstown, and Westminster was planned with a highway exchange less than three miles from campus. A rapid transit system from downtown Baltimore was in the works along the railroad right-of-way. Even the rural area of nearby McDonogh Road had been zoned for what would be at the time one of the East Coast's largest shopping malls, the Owings Mills Town Center.

The suburban explosion of the Reisterstown Road corridor was part of the Baltimore County Regional Planning Council's plan, but it was hardly what Garrison Forest envisioned. The encroaching development was an often-discussed, controversial topic at GFS trustee meetings, among faculty, and in carpool lines. Some expressed concern that remaining on Reisterstown Road surrounded by "high density housing and industry" meant a gradual slide into a day school only. Others felt that the school could "…move at great expense, to a new location only to find ourselves surrounded one day by something less desirable than what we have now." All agreed, though, that to attract boarding and day students *and* faculty, costly repairs to the campus' dilapidated buildings were sorely needed, as was professional prioritization about the school's needs. (As a result of the first GFS fundraising campaign in the 1950s, the Chapel, Meadowood dormitory, and an addition to Moncrieffe were built, but without any campus master plan.)

In 1966 came news of the county's plans to widen Garrison Forest Road into a four-lane highway and expand nearby Kenmar Road, a decision that would turn the campus into an "island" bordered by major roads. The trustees lobbied the county, but to no avail. In October 1966, the GFS board's executive committee unanimously agreed that the school would be best served by moving to another location away from development. But where and when? And just how much would it cost?

For answers, the board turned to the architectural/planning firm of Sasaki, Dawson & DeMay in summer 1967. Still weighing options to stay or move, the trustees requested cost estimates for modernizing the present campus for current and future needs and for moving and rebuilding elsewhere. After the firm came back with its estimates— $5 million to renovate and expand the

Reisterstown Road in the 1960s.

campus and $6 million to move—the trustees sought not one, but dozens of second opinions through a three-month, fact-finding mission.

Trustees Thomas Offutt, Miss Offutt's half-brother and an industrial realtor, Cornelia Rowland Levering '39, and Relie Garland Bolton '53 met with faculty, alumnae, parents, students, school administration past and present, community members in the Greenspring Valley and the St. Thomas' congregation, state planners, and local business leaders. Each group expressed a similar appreciation for the school's spirit of simplicity and humility, but staunch differences of opinion arose when the idea of moving the campus was broached. Many wanted to preserve the tradition of a more rural campus, and most agreed that the existing buildings were in terrible condition. Faculty opinion was either sentimental or practical. Several teachers, including Miss Brown and Mrs. Whitman, voiced concern over leaving or renovating the campus, which they found charming. However, Mrs. Vanderveer, Miss Simpson, Miss Porter, and Mr. Elliott concurred that the antiquated facilities *were* the problem, not current or future road patterns. It was "probably more sensible to move," they felt. The surrounding neighborhood, though, recalled Relie, "…was dead against GFS moving from Reisterstown Road."

Showing school spirit in 1967.

Recess on Manor House porch.

Greta McDonald Anderson '74 skipping in front of the Infantry in 1967. Lower School students (grades five through eight) in the 1950s and '60s used the aging building for classrooms.

Many of the issues discussed during these meetings—among them, coordinate education with other schools, a strict college preparatory program, and the use of technology—would become frequent faculty and board topics of discussion in coming years. The subcommittee's findings to the board recommended neither staying nor going, but urged further examination of the issue while engaging an architect and looking for new properties and property adjacent to the current campus. By April 1967, Baltimore County had abandoned its plans to expand Garrison Forest Road and Kenmar Avenue. Major road or not, the trustees felt that development was making an irrefutable and irreparable mark on Garrison Forest School. However, either choice—remain or relocate—required money the school did not have.

On January 15, 1968, a few days after the fact-finding committee presented its findings, the board received another blow. Mr. Montgomery announced his resignation, effective at the end of the academic year. He had received an unexpected offer to be headmaster of the Hill School, a boys' boarding school in Pottstown, Pennsylvania. Though not looking for another career opportunity, he felt he saw where the future of his beloved Garrison Forest was leading: farther into the country and further away from a boarding school. "Anita and I felt it was financially impossible to move," he recalled. "We saw Garrison Forest in a very special light… [and] felt moving out into the country was going to change a certain emphasis. Also, the notion of leading a boys' school was still in my head."

While the board searched for Mr. Montgomery's successor, another consulting firm, McKee-Berger-Mansueto, Inc., spent the winter crunching numbers, interviewing stakeholders, and scouring Baltimore County development plans and maps. Initially, this firm was inclined to recommend staying put "…because of the very real worry that Garrison's unique quality, its spirit, its aura…" might be lost in a move. However, the firm concluded in April 1968 that the "unnamed, but nevertheless real, quality is transferrable." Further, they determined that the school did not have sufficient holdings to stave off development and to maintain the desired on-campus environment, particularly for the boarding students. Given the high-density commercial industrial development surrounding the school, moving, it determined, was the best option.

During the May 3, 1968, board meeting, the trustees bid a fond and gracious farewell to the Montgomerys. At that meeting, with trustees on both sides of the fence, the board also voted to move, thus putting in place one of the most difficult and divisive chapters in Garrison Forest's history. Mr. Montgomery, who died in October 2009, and Mrs. Montgomery would remain close to the school and their students in the decades after their departure.

Mr. Montgomery and his students.

SPIRITED INTELLECT

Class, circa 1960s.

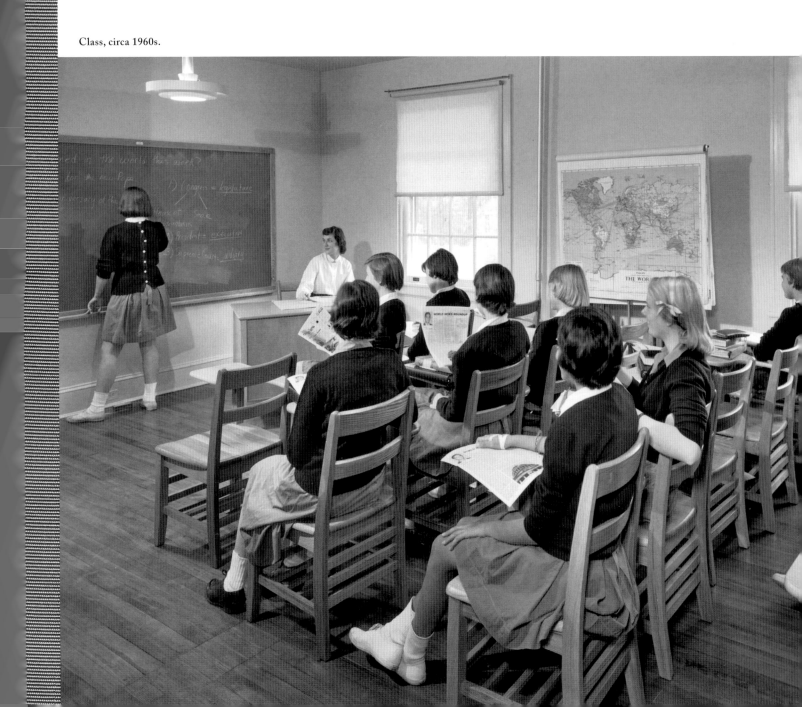

Garrison Forest School was a place of rigor from the beginning. With a vision of having a college preparatory school for girls at a time when the notion of girls attending college was relatively new, if not revolutionary, Miss Livingston set about creating a curriculum that would challenge her young students academically and instill in them strength of character and compassion for others. True to her mission, when Garrison Forest graduated its first two students in 1914, the two-member class passed the Bryn Mawr College entrance exam, the exam most young women sat for if they intended to attend college. Having the first two graduates of Garrison Forest pass an exam widely considered to be more difficult than Harvard's entrance exam was a badge of honor for the fledgling school.

A hallmark of Garrison Forest is its ability to be rooted to its founding vision—and the founding disciplines of languages, history, the arts, mathematics, and science courses—while remaining in the present day. As such, the school's curriculum has been at the vanguard of education at several points throughout its history. In 1948, when Miss Marshall and Miss Offutt closed the Infantry to focus on the education of girls beyond the primary grades, they created the Lower School for fifth through eighth grade to meet the unique intellectual, social, and emotional needs of middle-school-aged girls. At the time, and for the next few decades, having a specific program for middle grade students was unheard of in private, parochial, or public education. From 1948-75, Garrison Forest's program served only girls from fifth through twelfth grades. In 1975, the school merged with The Valley School and returned to its founding roots as a preschool through twelfth grade, while adding a further educational distinction with The Valley School's groundbreaking pre-first curriculum, which was among the first in the country.

Experiential learning has been part of the GFS program since 1969 through the Independent Senior Project (ISP), which was among the first of its kind in the Baltimore region. In 2005, the school expanded hands-on learning opportunities with the introduction of the Women in Science and Engineering (WISE) partnership with The Johns Hopkins University. Created as a response to the United States' dearth of female scientists and engineers, WISE offers GFS juniors and seniors the opportunity to enjoy a mentored internship in Hopkins' labs. In 2008, Garrison Forest received one of five innovative leadership grants from the E.E. Ford Foundation to establish the James Center: Programs and Partnerships with a Public Purpose. Named for trustee Amie Boyce James '70, who matched the Ford Foundation's challenge grant, the James Center encompasses the school's programs in community service, experiential learning, leadership development, and financial literacy.

AGE OF TECHNOLOGY

Garrison Forest welcomed the Technological Age in 1954 with a donation of typewriters. In 1972, the school leased its first computer, a Univac 1108, a behemoth that lived on the Manor House sun porch. Students programmed punch cards via a modem to a nearby college or university's mainframe. A year later, the school purchased its first computer, and by the early 1980s, all students had access to a computer room with nearly a dozen Apple IIe's donated by the Parent Association. During the 1990s, GFS added more computer labs and a digital library catalog. The 21st century heralded a fully wired campus and Tablet PC program for fourth through twelfth grades, and in 2009, Garrison Forest ventured into online learning with a pilot course for Advanced Placement (AP) French.

ROBOTICS

A part of its pre-engineering program, Garrison Forest began sponsoring robotics clubs for fourth through twelfth grade in the mid-2000s. Teams build and program robots to compete locally and statewide. In 2009, the fourth and fifth grade robotics team placed second in Creative Presentation in a Maryland state competition.

INDEPENDENT SENIOR PROJECT

An enduring legacy of the Hlavacek era is the Independent Senior Project (ISP), which Mr. Hlavacek introduced in 1969. Among the first of its kind in the Baltimore independent school community, ISP offers seniors the opportunity to explore a field of particular interest during a three-week internship. Originally, the program was voluntary, but by 1971—and every year since—the ISP became a graduation requirement. "It was mandatory, but we wanted to do an ISP…we all looked forward to pursuing something independent," noted Laurie Ober Curtis '74, who spent her ISP with Baltimore City's Protective Services Division of Child Abuse and Neglect.

Leigh McDonald Hall '81, GFS physical education teacher since 1996, traveled to a Navaho and Hope reservation in Tuba City, Arizona. She assisted Richard Hansen, M.D., a Baltimore plastic surgeon, while he performed pro-bono surgeries. The daughter of the late Joan McDonald, Middle School Latin teacher from 1975-85, Leigh was the first female to accompany Dr. Hansen on his annual trip. She logged several surgical hours, even assisting with a birth, experiences that inspired a nursing career in home healthcare. "My ISP gave me a perspective of other people's lives and struggles, and made me think about how governments' decisions affect people," Leigh said. "I had an opportunity to see different kinds of nursing, and I learned not to be intimidated when entering someone else's culture, life, or neighborhood." Poppy Hall '07 (right, second from left), Leigh's daughter, and Samantha Bloom '07 spent their ISP working in Nigeria with a physician from Presidents Emergency Plan for AIDS Relief (PEPFAR). They assisted an orphanage, clinic, AIDS hospital, and a daycare for mentally challenged and abused children. "Mom always said that ISP is a great time in your life to do something special, and I knew her [ISP] had been important to her," Poppy said. "My ISP made me realize how much I take for granted."

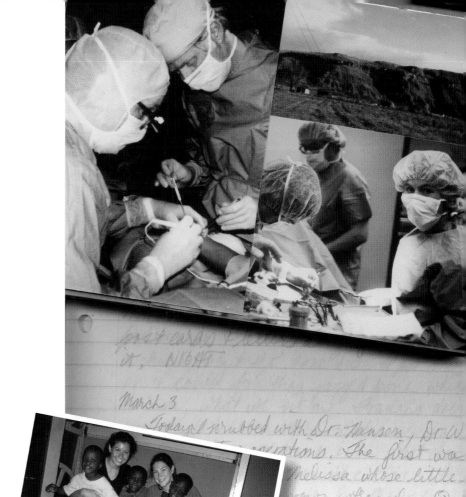

Leigh Hall's ISP photos and journal (above). Middle photo: Poppy Hall (left) and Samantha Bloom (right).

TRIPS

Academic field trips and off-campus programs have been part of the Garrison Forest curriculum since March 4, 1929, when teachers took the Upper School girls to Washington, D.C. to witness the inauguration of President Herbert Hoover. Ever since, girls have taken day and overnight trips to local, regional, and international destinations. In the 1980s the Upper School introduced QUEST—experiential overnight class trips to campgrounds, outdoor leadership ropes courses, and sometimes cities—for group bonding and to further class unity. Students also have enjoyed faculty-led international study trips since the 1970s to such locales as Spain, Russia, France, and England. The number of countries visited has expanded since 1995 to include Greece, Peru, Japan, China, and the Czech Republic.

Pictured above is a pre-first trip to the White House and, right, a Middle School trip to New York City.

Study Hall, 1968.

LAWRENCE L. HLAVACEK
HEADMASTER, 1968-1978

Lawrence "Larry" L. Hlavacek arrived in late June 1968, nearly two months after the school had made the decision to move its campus. He was fully aware and accepting of the decision and familiar with the controversy swirling around it. A new campus meant new challenges but also opportunities. As he settled into Lochinvar with his family—wife Linda, daughter Liza, 13, son Rusty, 11, a couple of cats, and a Basset hound named Shamus—he prepared to usher Garrison Forest into a new chapter, while readying for issues beyond the school's choice of location.

Change was everywhere. The headlines the first few weeks of September told of more bloodshed in Vietnam and more unrest at home, of Richard M. Nixon's selection for the Republican presidential ticket, of the Chicago Democratic convention marked by protestors and police brutality, of Hubert Humphrey's candidacy. "...The Vietnam War was in full swing; drugs hit the college and high school campuses with a vengeance; riots, protests, sit-ins abounded all over the country," noted the Rev. Marnie Knowles Keator '59 in her 2009 reunion weekend remarks during Chapel. "In spring 1968, within weeks of each other, Martin Luther King, Jr. and Robert Kennedy were gunned down. By the fall of that year, when students returned to school or college, there were suddenly no more norms...Gone were the clear expectations or clearly mapped out directions. Instead, we had to find our way amidst a culture that now had myriad options/choices, many of which we did not understand."

The late 1960s ushered in a new era on campuses across the country, college and otherwise. "The whole tenor of life was an unsteady one," noted Linda Hlavacek Silver, who remarried after Mr. Hlavacek died at the age of 70 in 1992. "When people ask me how long Larry's tenure was at Garrison, my answer always is '25 years.' All of us were ill prepared. We had no experience when students asked about marijuana or birth control pills or why they had to go to church on Sundays. Maybe these discussions had been had singularly [in the past], but not as a group." [Editor's note: For the section about the Hlavaceks' time at Garrison Forest, Mrs. Silver will be referred to as "Mrs. Hlavacek."]

(Left to right) Rusty, Larry, Liz, and Linda Hlavacek with Shamus, their dog

In the 1970s, it was all about the hair. Most teenaged girls and guys grew their hair long, a trend that younger kids often emulated. Irvin D. McGregor, Garrison Forest's cook and legend in the kitchen from 1965 to 2008, recalled a Saturday morning when a pre-teen, long-haired Rusty Hlavacek ran into the walk-in storage in Manor House. Mr. McGregor—all students and adults referred to him as "Irvin"—was putting food away after breakfast. "Larry was chasing Rusty to try to get him to get a haircut," chuckled Mr. McGregor. Rusty ran into the walk-in and hid. Neither he nor Mr. McGregor said anything, and Mr. McGregor continued what he was doing. Soon, Mr. Hlavacek burst through the same door and asked if Rusty had come through the walk-in. "I pointed to the outside door and said that I thought he went through there." Mr. Hlavacek uttered his thanks and ran outside. After a long silence, Mr. McGregor heard Rusty come out of his hiding place. "He mumbled some thanks and snuck out." When asked if Rusty ever re-ceived a haircut, Mr. McGregor just smiled: "Not that day."

Mr. Hlavacek, though, had ample experience with independent and boarding schools. After receiving his bachelor's degree from Wesleyan and his master's degree from Columbia, the Manhattan native taught history at Trinity School and Governor Dummer Academy before teaching and coaching for 21 years at The Lawrenceville School. His easy laugh and calm demeanor helped Garrison Forest ride the waves of change as they crested over the campus and country. It was his quiet leadership and ability to approach the issues unemotionally that impressed Elinor Purves McLennan '56 when she became a GFS trustee in 1973. "He wasn't pompous and got along with everybody," said Elinor, who was president of the board from 1986-89 and is now trustee Emerita.

The Headmaster and Mrs. Hlavacek
and
The Class of 1970
of
The Garrison Forest School
request the pleasure of your company
for
The Senior Dance Weekend
February 20th-22nd, 1970
Garrison, Maryland

EMBRACING OLD TRADITIONS

Mr. Hlavacek immediately endeared himself to the Garrison girls by gamely wearing a school tunic during New Girl week. The week's theme was "ballerina," and he bravely donned the tunic "tutu" of the other new students. At the request of a senior, he even pirouetted into Prayers. Mr. Hlavacek did inadvertently raise the ire of the longer-tenured faculty during his first faculty meeting, though, when he posed the question of whether the longstanding tradition of a mint julep party during Commencement festivities for families, faculty, and students was a wise idea. "You would have thought that he wanted to take every building to the ground," recalled Mrs. Hlavacek. The faculty insisted that it remain part of the festivities, which it did until the mid-1980s.

The community embraced Mrs. Hlavacek for her equally warm and approachable nature. She was a constant, cheerful presence on campus. "Larry and Linda were a team, and she was the energy behind him," noted Stuart Rinehart Stewart '66. "Linda had the details of life, and she knew every person on campus, knew their life history." The campus was less enthusiastic of Shamus' congenial nature. The dog blissfully lumbered around campus all day, searching for food with tail wagging and ears dragging—and a never-ending trail of shiny slobber in his wake. His drooling proficiency became so well-known that in May 1972, for the first Faculty Follies, Judy Reynolds, one of the faculty organizers for the show, recalled Mrs. Hlavacek dressing as Shamus with tinsel taped to her mouth to represent the dog's most distinctive feature.

The Hlavaceks continued several GFS traditions and started a few of their own. Like the Montgomerys before them, they hosted senior boarders at Lochinvar and other classes on other nights of the week. They introduced several holiday traditions, including a Halloween costume party complete with a pitch-black walk from Senior House, past the Chapel, and through the woods to Lochinvar. "The girls would scream all the way up the hill and all the way back down," laughed Mrs. Hlavacek. Another holiday favorite was the freshman party to decorate the Hlavaceks' Christmas tree and the seniors' Twelfth Night party to undecorate it. "We really encouraged the closeness of GFS," Mrs. Hlavacek said. Athletic teams, student concert performers, drama production casts, trustees, faculty, and staff all were frequent guests at Lochinvar.

Shamus was a constant presence on campus, especially during mealtimes.

Mr. Hlavacek dressed as a ballerina for "New Girl" week during his first year.

Decorating the Lochinvar Christmas tree.

Circa 1970s.

As a music lover, Mr. Hlavacek made sure the girls had ample opportunity to hear his favorite genre, with trips to jazz concerts and at school assemblies. In the mid-1970s, American composer Aaron Copland spent a week on campus as a guest lecturer and houseguest of the Hlavaceks. During Father/Daughter Weekend, a popular Hlavacek-era tradition, a jazz band played at a Saturday night dance at Lochinvar or the New Gym. The Hlavaceks also introduced the idea of families having a more formal role in the life of the school. In 1971-72, the Parent Association was founded, followed a few years later with the first Grandparents' Day, both traditions that continue today.

"Larry and Linda were married to the school," recalled Carol Peabody, who taught English from 1974 to 2002 and later returned as a part-time teacher until 2008. "Larry always stood in the Garland Theater lobby before a play or other performance to see what faculty showed up. Everyone knew that you went, and if you didn't it was a special reason. Of the heads during my tenure, he was right out of the tradition of novels of private schools. I give the Hlavaceks a lot of credit."

TO MOVE OR NOT TO MOVE

Mr. Hlavacek began his tenure fully accepting of the pending campus move. "That was a huge challenge for him to come and shepherd [the move]," said Relie Garland Bolton '53. "I recall him being enthusiastic about moving." Alumnae, faculty, and parents were divided on the issue, and while Green Spring Valley neighbors voiced concern, trustee Tom Offutt insisted in a 1968 *Baltimore Sun* interview that the school would not "move and leave a vacuum that will weaken the community." GFS Board President Nicholas G. Penniman III agreed, adding, "It will be many years before we actually move." In fact, consulting firm Sasaki, Dawson & DeMay had estimated that moving would take five to ten years.

Mr. Offutt and GFS Board Chairman J. Fife Symington, Jr. were assigned the task of finding suitable property, and the Reisterstown Road property was put on the market. That summer, Relie received a phone call that would eventually alter the course of the move. St. Timothy's School, an all-girls' boarding school in nearby Stevenson, approached her about coordinate education. Still exploring every option, the GFS board's new Planning and Development Committee met a few times with a similar committee from

St. Timothy's. In fact, such meetings were frequent occurrences among independent schools across the country during the late 1960s. For many schools, coordinate programs offered opportunities for increased course listings, students, and facility improvements.

For single-sex schools in particular, coordinate education represented an alternative to coeducation, a trend that swept through the nation's independent schools in the 1970s and 80s. By the mid-1970s, only 34 percent of the nation's independent schools would remain single sex, a significant drop from 64 percent a decade earlier. After a handful of cordial meetings during which the conversation steered from coordination to a merger, it was mutually decided, at that point, that the two schools should not combine, "...but [keep] their minds open to collaboration in various areas." The consulting firm urged the school to continue discussions regarding possible coordination while pursuing the campus move.

By early fall, Mr. Offutt and Mr. Symington had found what they felt was a suitable, if not perfect, place to relocate Garrison Forest: the 142-acre Timber Ridge Farm on Geist Road. The property easily met the trustee's stipulations with its rolling farmland overlooking the Western Run Valley, quaint buildings (including a large residence equipped with a generator and bomb shelter, the latter de rigueur in the Cold War environment of the 1960s), and no commercial development in sight. Negotiations began to purchase the Geist Road property for $400,000, and the trustees forged ahead with plans to move Garrison Forest deeper into the country.

By November, the school's offer to purchase the Geist Road property was accepted, and Mr. Penniman stepped down from leading the full board and into Chairman of the Executive Council. Mr. Symington was named Chairman of the Board—a new position—and Relie was named President. Hers was a historic appointment: she was the first woman and alumna to be named President of the GFS board. "Fife was heir apparent after Nick's retirement," Relie said. "Nick [Penniman] wanted to retire and thought the time had come for a woman [to lead] the board. Being president was something I thought I could do, but I was not angling for the job. At my age, I did not think that they would ask me." At the time of her appointment, she was a 33-year-old stay-at-home mother with one career experience under her belt: following graduation from Vassar, she had been an assistant to the curator and librarian at Baltimore's Walters Art Gallery.

Relie's appointment was, perhaps, the result of both nature and nurture. Her father, Charles S. Garland, had served as GFS Board President from 1951-57 and was Chairman of the Board of The Johns Hopkins University.

A brochure Garrison Forest produced describing the new campus. Students, faculty, and alumnae were bussed to Geist Road for occasional events, such as an alumnae reunion weekend picnic, during the time GFS owned the property.

This map, printed in a GFS fundraising brochure, shows the Geist Road property in relation to the Reisterstown Road campus.

The Geist Road property purchased by Garrison Forest in 1968 as the site of the new school.

The school breaks ground for the first Geist Road property buildings: faculty houses. Left to right: architect Avery Faulkner, Larry Hlavacek, Relie Bolton, and Tom Offutt.

Sister Courtney Garland Iglehart '48 and brother Charles S. Garland, Jr. also served as GFS trustees. A popular student, Relie was active in the GFS art and dramatics clubs and *Ragged Robin* editor-in-chief. Miss Gran playfully commented on her leadership abilities: "I hear noise in Shriver. I track it down. It is never Relie but just the natural confusion caused by the host of friends who follow her!"

The board had their work cut out for them: $6 million dollars was needed to build the new campus. The seemingly simple task of putting the Reisterstown Road campus up for sale—the rough asking price was $2 million—triggered heated trustee debate regarding re-zoning to commercial versus selling "as is." Communicating news of the move to alumnae, families, faculty, and neighbors was frequent and typically tense. Enrollment was holding somewhat steady, but the educational climate was changing. Garrison Forest and other girls' boarding schools were having difficulty competing as several formerly all-male boarding schools in the Northeast went coed. Fewer girls were choosing to attend boarding schools, and if they did, their choice was typically coed. In fall 1968, Garrison Forest's Education Committee discussed coeducation but voted to remain single-sex.

Then there was the small matter of the nation's growing economic crisis. Interest rates were at an all-time high in 1970 when the fundraising campaign for the move officially began. Any further borrowing—the school had already borrowed $400,000 to purchase the Geist Road property—was out of the question. Garrison Forest was operating at a loss with a $30,000 deficit projected for 1970-71. The school cut costs and put off all but the most pressing maintenance to its decrepit buildings, "holding [the campus] together by string and wire until the day of the move," as noted in board minutes. Raising faculty salaries could not be delayed. Higher salaries were needed immediately to recruit and retain faculty in a competitive, national market.

The board pressed ahead, launching a national competition to find an architect. Avery Faulkner, a highly respected architect and partner with Faulkner, Freyer and Vanderpool in Washington, D.C., was selected to design and build the new campus. Taking his design cues from the Geist Road property's rolling hills and history as a working farm, he designed a series of modern, wooden buildings inspired by Maryland bank barns. He dubbed his design a "hilltop educational village" comprising a town square, residential buildings, and spaces for art, music, and recreation. With a completion date set for 1972, the school broke ground for four faculty houses in May 1969.

As 1969 drew to a close, the school had raised only $350,000 in pledges to construct its new campus. Construction on faculty housing and site grading for athletic fields were underway, but the board could not move forward with the major new academic and residential buildings until more money was raised and the Reisterstown Road property was sold. Without commercial zoning, it would be difficult to find a serious buyer. Current expenses were pressing, including an immediate $85,000 needed to bring faculty salaries in line with regional schools, a sum financed by raising day students' tuition. The trustees could not in good conscience raise boarding tuition until the school moved. Mr. Faulkner estimated five years at most on the Reisterstown Road campus without any major improvements, and the board agreed that the "shabby appearance of the buildings will prevent [Garrison Forest] from attracting the type of student whom we want."

The new year brought good news as a serious buyer emerged who was willing to allow Garrison Forest to remain on the campus rent-free for three years. The buyer's plan was to create a commercial office park. The board began the arduous process of pressing Baltimore County for re-zoning the property to commercial use, but by early August 1970, the school's attorney, Thomas D. Washburne, announced that the buyer had withdrawn his offer.

Reisterstown Road development brought more opportunities for nearby off-campus jaunts, including trips to Baskin-Robbins™ across the street. It remains an after school destination in 2010.

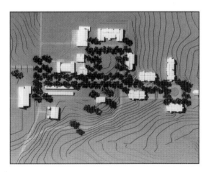

An aerial view of Avery Faulkner's architectural model showing his "hilltop educational village" for the Geist Road property.

Studying hard in 1971...

...and having fun outside of class.

The buyer cited that "…the school had waited entirely too long with respect for zoning." Petitions to alter the zoning map were due by the end of the month, a deadline the school could not meet. Disappointed, the trustees relisted the property. As the months pressed on without a serious buyer, the trustees knew that without commercial zoning for the entire campus, a buyer was unlikely—and the school desperately needed top dollar for its present campus in order to construct its new one.

Garrison Forest managed to raise another million for the building campaign—the total pledges stood at $1.3 million, a Herculean effort given the economy—but much more was needed to construct academic and residential buildings on the Geist Road campus. Several offers on the Reisterstown Road property had been made, but the ideal purchaser still eluded the school. From the start, the decision to move had been controversial within and beyond the GFS board, and the strain was starting to show. Several trustees resigned, among them Mr. Symington, who resigned in 1969 upon his appointment by President Richard M. Nixon as Ambassador to Trinidad and Tobago. Others, however, cited the move as the deciding factor. An alumna trustee wrote that she could not "…share the views of all who are so enthusiastic about the move." Three-term trustee J. Pierre Bernard wrote in his cordial resignation to GFS Board Chairman Raymond S. Clark, who succeeded Mr. Symington, that he was "…by nature, cautious and this may well be a time which calls for bold and aggressive action… These [trustee] positions should be held by those with a more positive feeling and greater confidence in our program."

Garrison Forest's struggles with its intended move were well known in the community. In early 1971, McDonogh School approached the trustees about merging, offering GFS land at the back of the McDonogh campus but with no prospect of sharing facilities. Both schools had strong cultures, and after 12 civil meetings, the schools questioned whether their cultures could co-exist. "We listened to McDonogh and came away feeling that Garrison Forest would be swallowed up," recalled Relie. "We advised them to start their own girls' school," she said of Garrison Forest's decision to end conversations with McDonogh, which became coed in 1975.

It was during this time that Relie received another phone call from St. Timothy's. "They asked if rather than move, would we consider moving to their plant," Relie said. "We needed to consider every option. St. Tim's enrollment was down, and our campus was terrible." So was Garrison Forest's endowment, which hovered around $400,000. At the time, St. Timothy's had a $2.3 million endowment and a nice campus. Merging the schools would require an estimated $3.5 million for new buildings on St. Timothy's campus—half the cost of the Geist Road campus construction.

If moving Garrison Forest deeper into the country to Geist Road was controversial, talk of merging with another girls' school was incendiary. The trustees held meetings with faculty, alumnae, and students to discuss options, and though Relie recalled receiving letters both for and against the merger, the prevailing opinion beyond the board weighed on the side of staying put and making the best of it on the Reisterstown Road campus. Nancy Offutt was particularly vocal. In earlier board meetings, she had agreed with the decision to move the campus, but merging with another school was another matter entirely. Board records show little evidence of Miss Offutt's dissent during meetings, but her opposition buzzed across phone lines. "Miss Offutt was fighting it the entire time [by] calling alumnae, saying, 'Just don't let the merge happen,' " noted Relie. "It was a very conflicted situation, and here I was a 30-something trying to sort it all out." Meg Murray Keech '44, a trustee at the time, remembers Miss Offutt calling every alumna she could locate. "I heard her phone bill looked like the national debt when she was finished," Meg commented.

The idea of merging with St. Timothy's was hardly popular with faculty. A merger meant an amalgamation of faculty. "There was a lot of angst. We just didn't know what was going to happen," remembered Lorraine Polvinale, who was hired in 1971 as Garrison Forest's first full-time Spanish teacher, and later served as head of the Middle School (1992-98) and head of the Upper School (1998-2007). "If we merged, we knew that some of us would lose our jobs." There also could only be one head of the merged school, and neither Mr. Hlavacek nor Jean Miller, his counterpart at St. Timothy's, was necessarily a lock. In all likelihood, Relie recalled, the merger meant a new hire for Head of School.

The pressure for a solution was mounting. At $1.8 million, campaign funds for the Geist Road campus were far below the now estimated $6.5-$7 million needed. The four faculty houses were built and occupied by GFS staff and teachers, but any further construction was put on hold. Talks continued to be held with St. Timothy's, while the November 1971 decision date by Baltimore County on the school's commercial re-zoning application loomed. And Garrison Forest's indecision to stay or go was taking its toll, Mr. Hlavacek reported to the board. Some students were going elsewhere; some parents were not contributing because of the school's uncertain future; and the present plant was in desperate need of repair. "Money is our problem," he stated simply. To examine the present challenges and set a

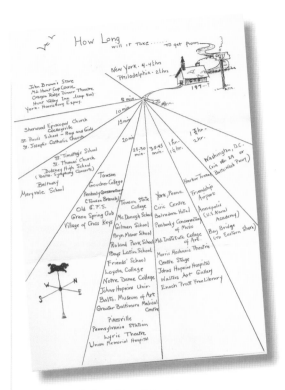

A map designed by GFS to show alumnae and families how close the new campus would be.

In front of Robinswood.

September 22, 1971
Garrison Forest School
Garrison, Maryland

Board of Trustees
Garrison Forest School
Garrison, Maryland

Ladies and Gentlemen of the Board:

I would most respectfully like to submit to the Board of Trustees the results of a student body poll taken on the 21 and 22 September. These figures come after a meeting of the students from grades 8 through 12 with Mrs. Bolton, and after a series of informal discussion periods between the students, faculty, and administration.

We hope our activities of this past week have demonstrated our sincere interest in the well being of Garrison Forest School, and we feel confident that after extensive consideration of the St. Timothy-Garrison question, the Board will reach the most suitable answer to our present situation.

Thank you so very much.

Sincerely yours,

Liza Bailey
Pres. of the Student Body

Enclosure

President of the School Liza Bailey Musgrave '72 presented Relie Bolton with this letter and results of a student petition (below) to be read at the September 1971 trustee meeting.

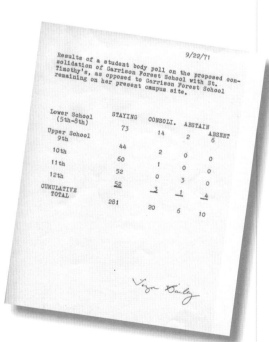

9/22/71

Results of a student body poll on the proposed consolidation of Garrison Forest School with St. Timothy's, as opposed to Garrison Forest School remaining on her present campus site.

	STAYING	CONSOLI.	ABSTAIN	ABSENT
Lower School (5th-8th)	73	14	2	6
Upper School 9th	44	2	0	0
10th	60	1	0	0
11th	52	0	3	0
12th	52	3	1	4
CUMULATIVE TOTAL	281	20	6	10

Liza Bailey

course for Garrison Forest, in April 1971, the board appointed its first long-range planning committee, which Mr. Hlavacek had long championed.

In her summer 1971 progress report to the school community, Relie wrote of invitations by both McDonogh and St. Timothy's to relocate to their campuses and of the frustrating zoning delays for the Reisterstown Road campus. "These delays have given all of us a chance to restudy ourselves, to check our course and to conclude once again that Garrison Forest is indeed a rare place. With all the indecision this year has held, this school has kept her strength, her serenity, and her sense of humor."

In July 1971, the trustees convened a special meeting to discuss possible consolidation with St. Timothy's. Several faculty members and alumnae were invited guests. The GFS committee that had been meeting with representatives from St. Timothy's unanimously recommended the merger for several reasons, among them: "certain academic possibilities heretofore prohibited by dollars and cents" including a postgraduate year, coordinate seminars with local boys' schools, and a broader curriculum. Other advantages included St. Timothy's endowment and campus versus an entirely new campus needed at Geist Road. At the meeting, Mr. Hlavacek was asked his preference to consolidate if he were headmaster of the merged school or of a re-developed Reisterstown Road campus. He replied that he would carry out whatever decision the board made, though he noted the "the negative opinion of some trustees and of all alumnae who contacted him regarding consolidation" and of the "…toll that the uncertainty is taking on the school."

The meeting lasted six hours, ending in a show of hands with 17 of the 25 voting members in favor of consolidation, but only with Mr. Hlavacek as the head of the new school. Were Mr. Hlavacek not chosen as head of the merged school, 21 trustees voted in favor of remaining on Reisterstown Road. All agreed that because of accelerating building costs and an inability to raise the necessary funds, the Geist Road property was no longer practical.

After the meeting, Relie explained to Percy H. Clark, Jr., President of the St. Timothy's Board, that GFS felt that the head of the new school should be named upon consolidation approval. Further, she noted that Garrison Forest should have the right to select the head as part of the merger agreement. Mr. Clark suggested a compromise of a 10-member Executive Committee (five members from each school) empowered to select the head, reiterated St. Timothy's offer of consolidation, and set a fall deadline for Garrison Forest's decision.

On September 22, 1971, the opening trustee meeting for the 1971-72 year, Relie arrived at the meeting in Meadowood with two letters to read: one if the GFS board voted to merge; the other if it voted to stay. During the meeting,

she read a petition to remain on the Reisterstown Road campus signed
by 87 percent of the GFS faculty. A letter from Liza Bailey Musgrave '72,
President of the School, and later, GFS trustee, showed the result of a
student poll, with the overwhelming majority in favor of not merging with
St. Timothy's. "Being a rabble-rouser, from day one, I was against [the
merger]," recalled Liza. "Both were fine schools, each with a sense of its
own traditions. They were just very different."

Trustees for and against the merger voiced their opinions during the
meeting, and then Miss Offutt spoke. "Garrison Forest today on the present
campus and the problems of continuation during the Great Depression,"
were similar, she said, and she stated her conviction that "the determined
spirit of the 1930s will persist in the development of the school on…Reis-
terstown Road." A motion was made and seconded to approve consolidation with St. Timothy's in principle. Then, through a roll call, each trustee
announced his or her vote. With 12 ayes and 22 nays, the trustees voted
against the proposed merger with St. Timothy's. Shortly after the vote,
the board voted to change all votes to reflect a unanimous vote against the
merger. Discussing the vote decades later, Relie expressed surprise that it
was not closer: "The Executive Committee was all in favor, save one
person…We did not know until roll call who was for or against it. We
thought we would prevail in the end, but we did not."

With the appropriate letter in hand, Mr. Hlavacek walked to Study Hall
to share the results with the students, and Relie called St. Timothy's with
the news. After hearing the news, several students continued on to
Evenlode for a scheduled pre-dinner meeting with Mr. Elliott to hammer
out the finishing touches on a new student government constitution. As the
students discussed the board's decision, they decided to show their
appreciation to the trustees who were dining at Lochinvar. The students
and faculty on campus walked to the headmaster's house. Standing on the
lawn in front of the stone steps, the group serenaded the Hlavaceks and
trustees with the strains of "Hail Gladdening Light." They walked back
down the hill singing "Rise and Shine," serenaded a few faculty houses,
and then proceeded to Manor House for ice cream and doughnuts. The last
stop of the evening was the Chapel where the trustees joined them, and
Mr. Hlavacek offered a prayer of thanks and hope for the future. Following
more singing, the boarders dispersed to the dorms, hoarse but happy.

"It was very emotional, and the trustees were touched that the students
said 'thank you,'" Mrs. Hlavacek reflected. "The move to Geist Road
and the merger were rough things and distracted everyone." Liza agreed:
"Everyone that whole fall was exhausted over it."

Hanging out in the dormitory, circa 1960s.

The Garrison Forest School
Garrison, Maryland
21055

Dear Miriam – Especially for you!
September 24, 1971

To the Board of Trustees of the Garrison Forest School:

I want to personally thank you all for your hard work,
concern for and devotion to our school. The past few
months have not been easy ones. The very future of
Garrison Forest, in particular, and of independent schools,
in general, was uppermost in everyone's thoughts.

You were of diverse opinions of what course we should
follow. You were divided, honestly, in what action should
be taken at the present time. Yet, your motive was one –
to preserve the unique qualities of Garrison Forest.

When the decision to remain at our present site was
reached, painstakingly and thoughtfully, you all
concurred in a spirit of typical selflessness and goodwill.

I am honored and proud to be associated with you. I am
expecially grateful to Garrison Forest for letting Linda
and me be part of it.

Sincerely,

Larry

Lawrence L. Hlavacek
Headmaster

LLH:mm

Miriam Vanderveer's copy of the
letter sent to all the trustees from
Mr. Hlavacek following the vote in favor
of remaining as Garrison Forest on
Reisterstown Road.

A drawing that appeared in *The Blueprint* following the board's vote in September 1971.

The Blueprint headline following the vote.

"I remember that alumnae could not be brought to the table on moving, that was what it boiled down to," noted Ginny Gaillard Chew, '48, who served on the board during that time. "The merger had a more emotional reaction, that GFS would lose its identity. Relie bore the brunt of a lot and took it on the chin to lead us forward. On balance, staying was the right decision. There was a lot of pride that...we did not need St. Tim's or a beautiful new campus to be Garrison Forest. People just dug in and made it work." In the months that followed, the school immediately began redesigning the Reisterstown Road campus with plans for a new stable and indoor riding ring, Upper School and Middle School academic buildings, and Garland Theater, a performing arts center named for Charles S. Garland, who had died unexpectedly in January 1971, just as the merger talks began.

"It was a bitter time," said Relie of her years as board president during such a fractious period. In 1972, she stepped down as president to serve four years as chair of the education committee. "During the move and merger years, the board's executive committee was so supportive. Mrs. Van even sent me notes in Latin. I love Garrison Forest—my sister and I went here and all our daughters and nieces have gone through—and that got me through such a wild time. I did it by sheer guts. I learned that you always have to consider your options. In the 1970s, so many things were at stake. It was hard to get it right."

Nearly four decades after the monumental decision to remain as a stand-alone school on Reisterstown Road, Garrison Forest has transformed its 110-acre campus into a blend of historic buildings and new facilities designed in the school's architectural vernacular. "The campus is another example of Garrison Forest's resilience and ability to reinvent itself," noted G. Peter O'Neill, Jr., head of school since 1994. "In 1971, the school had the courage to stay on this site and to take advantage of this location, which meant that it was in a better position to increase the enrollment among day students because of the increase in population around us and the growth in suburban areas outside Baltimore. We were very well positioned, and I think as a result, a very successful school today."

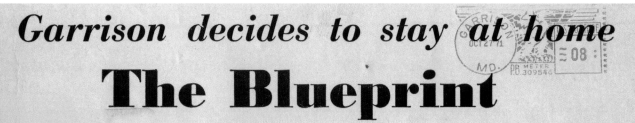

Garrison decides to stay at home
The Blueprint

GARRISON FOREST SCHOOL   October, 1971

Board votes unanimously to remain on present campus

The Board of Trustees of the Garrison Forest School de-

Playing with campus dogs on Manor House lawn.

Fun in the GFS fields.

NEGOTIATING CHANGING TIMES

With the decision to remain on Reisterstown Road, Garrison Forest's location may not have changed, but nearly everything else about life at the school—and the world outside the campus—was changing. Garrison Forest students at the time may have been more genteel in their approach than their national counterparts, but the idea of questioning authority—and everything else—was the same. Pamela Achilles Gould '73 remembers her freshman fall at GFS in 1969, and feeling the ripple effect of Woodstock, the debut of the Broadway musical *Hair*, and continuing escalation in Vietnam. "We had older siblings who had been drafted, were waiting to find out their [draft] number, or were dodging the draft," she said. "A lot of the change in the air was anger, which I think, affected the freshman class. We were not going to settle for the school being strict and having only three weekends [away] and dresses measured three inches from our knees."

The freshmen and other students voiced their discontent to Mr. Hlavacek and the seniors, and subsequently the number of weekends doubled. And for the first time since uniforms were introduced during the Marshall-Offutt era, the school stopped measuring skirt length. But wearing uniforms at a then-fashionable miniskirt length was still not allowed. As a protest, Nancy Sullivan '71 let out all hems so that her uniform skirts were at least mid-calf and wore paddock boots instead of the traditional lace-up brown oxfords. "The [uniform] code said we were to wear brown lace-ups so I was just pushing the envelope a little."

Cheerleaders in 1973.

1970s

The Chapel Bell holds historic and spiritual significance. Given in 1950 by the Shriver family in memory of George M. Shriver, the school's longest-tenured board president, and his son, Charles M. Shriver, who succeeded his father as president, the bell is the engine bell for the last steam locomotive of the Baltimore & Ohio Railroad. Engraved on the bell's plaque are the words, "Give me beauty in the inward soul and may the outward and inward man be as one"—words that have resonated with generations of Garrison girls.

1950s

Questioning the school's uniform restrictions was a way to question the status quo. One student wore her tunic inside out nearly every day and tied her belt around her head, still within the stated rules. Apparently, during the era of bra burning, some girls chose not to wear bras for feminist statement, hippie fashion, or personal preference. Mrs. Hlavacek remembered a few parents stopping her husband on school mornings to insist that he "get the girls to wear underwear." Rather than reprimand certain sartorial statements, he calmly asked the parents how they intended he do that, noting that if the dorm residents checked for bras—one of the parents' suggestions—the students would just take them off later.

The 1970s was an era of contradictions, though. Joan Smith, who was hired to teach French in 1967 before serving as dean of students and then school counselor from 1981-93, remembered little outward rebellion with uniforms. Though skirt measuring may have ceased, uniform regulations were still in place, she noted. Randie Mulholland Benedict '76 and director of admissions from 1990 to 2009, concurred: "Blue knee socks had to be straight. I wore rubber bands around the top of the socks [to keep them up.]. In the Middle School, Miss Taylor held daily white shoe inspection. We had white roll-on shoe polish for our boat shoes."

Students yearned for—and received—more freedom during the Hlavacek era. Juniors could now study in their dormitory rooms in the evening and drive with day students. Younger boarders could now venture off campus for weekend shopping trips and older girls enjoyed a later "lights out." Said Caroline Johnson Patterson '71, "I always felt that the Hlavaceks gave us attention and respect."

Linda and Larry Hlavacek shared the majority of boarders' opinion that mandatory attendance at St. Thomas' on Sunday morning and for evening Vespers in the Chapel was too much. By 1970, attendance at either was voluntary, though later in the decade, Mr. Hlavacek instituted compulsory Sunday Vespers attendance for boarders once a month. Whether voluntary or mandatory, Chapel on Sundays and periodic, student-led Wednesday night Vespers services were popular, noted Pamela Gould. "Whatever was going on, which was a lot, Chapel was a peaceful time that united us spiritually," she reflected.

Students and faculty could express concerns and ideas to the GFS trustees through elected student and faculty representatives to the board, an idea championed by Mr. Hlavacek in 1968. Representatives, however, attended the meeting only during their report. Rev. James Hammond, who succeeded Rev. Thomas S. Baker as school chaplain and chair of the (one-person) religion department, arrived in summer 1974 during the Watergate hearings. "I remember thinking to myself that we were living in a very tumultuous time.

The mood on the campus of Garrison Forest, as I remember it, on arrival, was one of some tension. Some members of the faculty desired to discuss openly all of the issues of the day, not only in the context of current events, but also in the greater context of how life should be lived. Whether the more global issues were at the forefront of daily life of the school might be a matter of debate, but certainly it is true to say that there was some unrest on the campus between trustees, administration, faculty, and the student body on local, certainly more mundane issues of day-to-day life for the young women."

At the dawn of the 1970s, students also began hosting town meetings on a regular basis to engage the school community in discussing the issues affecting Garrison Forest. Under the guidance of humanities teacher Don Elliott, in 1971-72 the Student Government Association renamed itself Forum and wrote and ratified the first-ever Constitution for Garrison Forest's student government. In addition to formalizing student government operations, the constitution clarified the rights of students.

Though student behavior at Garrison Forest was certainly tame given the radicalism at the time on college and high school campuses nationwide, a rebel spirit did exist. Students staged a sit-in to prevent trees from being cut down for the construction of Marshall-Offutt, the new academic building for the Upper School. Perhaps the greatest sign of the times, though, was the short-lived *Trueprint*, an underground student newspaper.

While the paper's exact genesis cannot be confirmed, on January 22, 1973, the first and what would be the only issue circulated throughout the school. The anonymous articles included a fable about the village of Nosirrag (Garrison spelled backwards) and its inhabitants (thinly-veiled caricatures of administrators and faculty). At the time, no students or faculty claimed responsibility for publication or planting the idea. A *Blueprint* editorial published shortly thereafter noted that there was "…more controversy over who published the [paper] than over its message." Though *Blueprint* editors commended the *Trueprint*'s "forthright manner in which the problems of the school were presented," they urged specific solutions in future issues. "The *Trueprint* certainly stirred passions on both sides of the issue. Nothing constructive was offered by the students to remedy the criticisms," concurred Terry Chase, Ph.D., who served as history department chair and dean of faculty.

Later that spring, Pamela Gould and two friends decided to boycott the U.S. History exam. "We were talking among ourselves about what is universal truth," said Pamela. Determining that the regurgitation of facts was not the true nature of education, the students approached Judy

In class.

Walking to Study Hall.

The first new construction project to be completed after the board's decision to remain on the Reisterstown Road campus was the Thomas and Elizabeth Sheridan Indoor Riding Ring and Stables, constructed in 1972. With the Sheridan Riding Ring, the school finally had the equestrian facilities to match the high level of its riding program. After the D. & J. Smith Equestrian Center was built in 1998, the Sheridan Riding Ring, which had been shared with polo, became the Indoor Polo Ring, to house the school's nationally recognized polo program.

In the 1970s, Garrison Forest participated in a local television show, *It's Academic*, produced by WJZ-Channel 11. Coached by history teacher Judy Reynolds (pictured standing top row left), the GFS team fielded trivia questions and competed against other local schools.

Reynolds, U.S. History teacher, with their decision, and then met with Mr. Hlavacek. "It was nothing against Judy," said Pamela. "We adored her and she really cared about us. It was just part of the nature of the times." Ms. Reynolds, who taught history and served as the college counselor from 1970-80, explained that the students who boycotted would receive a zero. The next day, during the exam, Pamela and the two others sat quietly at their desks with their heads down.

"Ironically, one of the questions was what would have happened had the South won the Civil War, a question that required all sorts of opinion and fact," Ms. Reynolds remarked. Over three decades later, Pamela reflected on the boycott and Ms. Reynolds' reaction as but one example of the closeness and openness between GFS students and faculty, even during such a fractious time nationally. "Garrison Forest really was an extended family," she said. "I cannot believe the tolerance the faculty had. We must have been such a pain to them."

Choosing his battles was a skill that served Mr. Hlavacek well during the challenges of the 1970s—a sign on his desk stated, "I SAID MAYBE"—and he often expressed to the trustees the new reality. "It is up to the administration and faculty to realize that the [students] are simply expressing a new way of life, which we must learn to understand," he wrote.

Drugs existed on campus but were not prevalent, though an unsigned letter to the editor in the March 1970 *Blueprint* warned readers of a local and federal law enforcement crackdown on drug buyers. Both Ms. Reynolds and Mrs. Smith chuckled at a student rumor in 1972. While the faculty secretly rehearsed the inaugural Faculty Follies in the Old Gym, students were convinced that these were really meetings between teachers and police to plan drug raids. "The seniors told me later that whatever [drugs were] on campus were flushed," said Ms. Reynolds.

Traditional school dances were still held, though the girls shook those up as well. Petitions circulated in 1972 asked for more dances and for the elimination of assigned dates. Liza Bailey Musgrave '72 recounted an invitation by the Naval Academy to attend a tea dance. "We raided the Garrison costume closet with Miss Jackson [Irene Jackson, dorm resident, who worked at GFS from 1949-89] and went as Gibson Girls. We were not invited back. I can't say we were crushed."

It was during this time that the school introduced more weekend activities for the boarders and day students beyond dances on campus and at boys' schools in Baltimore and the Mid-Atlantic region. Students went on school-sponsored camping and skiing trips, visited museums, and attended Baltimore

Orioles baseball games. They watched plays at Baltimore's Lyric Opera House and the Morris Mechanic Theatre and went to performances by a variety of performers—from Blood, Sweat & Tears and Emerson, Lake & Palmer to Benny Goodman and Johnny Cash.

During the 1970s, several long-term teachers retired, including Miss Gran, Miss White, Miss Brown, and Miss Boyd. For four years, Mr. Hlavacek succeeded in persuading Mrs. Vanderveer not to retire, which she had planned to do his first year. The two developed a close friendship and professional association. "Day in and day out, she was in his corner," said Mrs. Hlavacek. "She had this tweed suit, and if something had happened with the faculty, she would stand over Larry's desk and say, 'I've got my fighting suit on. Do you want me to get into this with the faculty?' Larry would say, 'Now, now, Miriam, calm down.'"

Colonial Day, pictured left in 1976, is a longstanding tradition at GFS. Each spring since the 1970s, the third grade dons period garb for a party culminating their study of Colonial times. (Photo above, 2004.)

```
STOP

READY

SCR

READY

5 PRINT "DAHLGREN---PROJECT 3"
10 LET B=0
15 READ A
16 DATA 1,67,-5,45,7,7,88,-99,18,3,9
20 DATA 2,6,77,4,3,5,-99,9,67,999999
25 IF A=999999 THEN 55
30 LET A-=-1
35 LET B=B+A
40 PRINT B
45 GO TO 15
55 LET C=0
55 READ A
56 DATA 1,67,-5,45,7,7,88,-99,18,3,9
57 DATA 2,6,77,4,3,5,-99,9,67,999999
55
56
57
```

The first GFS computer, which was housed on the Manor House sun porch.

Mr. Hlavacek introduced Upper School block courses in 1969, which were voluntary, exploratory classes in subjects such as child psychology, creative writing, typing, and ceramics. Though the idea only continued for a few years, in 2005 the Middle School adopted the idea into its Minimester program, a four-day exploration of interdisciplinary courses. The short hiatus from regular classes has included courses in forensic science, medieval calligraphy and block-printing, French cuisine, self-defense, and claymation (pictured above).

CURRICULUM CHANGES

Upon his arrival at GFS, Mr. Hlavacek recognized immediately the high level of teaching and learning at the school. He applied for a Cum Laude chapter, and in 1970, Garrison Forest was awarded membership in the Cum Laude Society. Founded nationally in 1906 and modeled after Phi Beta Kappa, the Cum Laude Society recognizes academic excellence, as well as good character and integrity in all areas of school life at the secondary school level. Since its inception at Garrison Forest, more than 310 students have been honored at an annual spring assembly, during which an alumna Cum Laude member addresses the Upper School. As further recognition of the academic abilities of the students, during the Hlavacek era the school introduced six Advanced Placement courses.

Students wanted more freedom in class—or at least in the type of courses offered. In his report to the board in May 1969, Mr. Hlavacek noted the students' desire for "more contemporary courses and closer contact with urban problems." For several years prior to his arrival, the faculty and trustees had been concerned with curriculum as part of the discussions about the campus move and merger with St. Timothy's. As a result, Latin was no longer a graduation requirement, and Spanish was a full-time subject, taught by Lorraine Polvinale, who joined GFS in 1971. Credit classes were offered in communications, sociology, music theory, and ceramics, and students could take a non-credit creative writing course at McDonogh. The voluntary, twice-a-week block classes that were added to the schedule in 1969-70 gave students even more choices, with classes in creative writing, ceramics, drama, child psychology, typing, The Negro in American Literature, and sewing, as well as religion and art history.

In 1972, the school took its first step into the Age of Technology with a leased computer located on the Manor House sun porch. The computer connected via modem to a local university or college, and under the tutelage of Peter Whiting, mathematics teacher, both Middle and Upper School students learned Beginner's All-Purpose Symbolic Instructional Code (BASIC) programming. The process involved storing the programs on paper punch tape, dialing into the university computer, feeding the tape through a reader, and running the program. Days later, the results would be transmitted back to GFS. "If there were problems, we would go off-line, debug, and try again," wrote Lee McShane Cox '78, who taught mathematics at Garrison Forest from 1983-87. A year later, Garrison Forest purchased its own computer.

By the end of the decade, the school also added another important dimension to the curriculum. Garrison Forest and many independent and public schools were beginning to recognize learning differences. In 1977, GFS hired two full-time reading specialists and the English department developed and taught a study skills program. "We began to understand dyslexia and other learning differences," said Mrs. Polvinale. "It was a slow, slow process to identify and evaluate these kids and to try a different way of teaching, but we knew that there had to be a better way to reach them. Garrison took a wide range of students and had a lot to offer a variety of levels of student. A lot of students with academic differences became our key leaders."

In 1972, GFS students took to the skies when math teacher, GFS Admissions director, and licensed pilot Miss Porter offered a private pilot ground course. The pilot aviation course covered skills needed to sit for a pilot's license, including flying regulations, reading flight charts, and understanding airplane mechanics.

A bumper sticker on campus (left).

UNREST AT HOME AND ABROAD

During the Vietnam War, evening television news brought the war home in vivid, tragic detail for boarders in the dorm common rooms and for day scholars in their homes. With several students' and teachers' family members fighting in Vietnam, the topic often was discussed in classes, particularly in history classes, Rev. Baker's Ethics class, and Mr. Elliott's classes, though Ms. Reynolds recalled few conversations in her history classes due to students' lack of interest. There were a couple of organized, peaceful protests on the GFS campus but not to the extent of the protests by many student counterparts across the country. "There had been a seminal shift when we were there," noted Liza Musgrave. "We were incredibly well-behaved young ladies, though. We weren't burning buildings."

Though there were no protests on campus, Garrison Forest students did express themselves politically in reaction to national and international events during the late 1960s and throughout the 1970s. Students attended rallies at other schools and protested in Washington, D.C., and *The Blueprint* included articles and editorial cartoons on the political and social issues of the day.

Did Nixon really know?

Of all the Upper School underclassmen and faculty the following participated in a poll on the Watergate situation.

No seniors participated; therefore, we excluded them in figuring the percentages.

Grade	9	10	11	Faculty	Totals
Board	5	4	12		21
Day	29	5	11	12	57
Total %	70	20	40	30	35

One Saturday evening during 1969-70, several of the dormitories began a spontaneous singing of the John Lennon/Yoko Ono refrain: "All we are saying is give peace a chance." The song was sung back and forth, dorm to dorm, for an hour, remembered Pamela Gould. The next year, Rev. Baker took a group of students in the GFS van to the White House in Washington, D.C. For an hour, the students silently and peacefully picketed on the sidewalk with signs asking the U.S. government to release the names of prisoners of war. Students also organized a day-long fast to show awareness and support of the suffering in Cambodia, which included an open forum in the Chapel to discuss the war.

The Blueprint published occasional articles on the war, and on October 15, 1969, the Upper School suspended classes to participate in the National Moratorium Day, a symbolic nationwide protest. The purpose of the event was to encourage teachers and students to leave campus for the day and go door-to-door to speak with Americans about the need for peace. Garrison Forest's participation, though, deviated from this plan. Students were obliged to attend classes in the morning, with some students choosing to dress in "dark clothes of mourning," as reported in *The Blueprint*. In the afternoon, teachers gathered outside in small groups with students to discuss the Vietnam War and issues of peace. In the evening, the senior class held further informal discussions, after which about three-quarters of the boarding community gathered in the Chapel for a reflective, student-led service of readings and songs.

Not all awareness was global, however. Kathryn Noel Phillips '70 remembered Miss Brown addressing an assembly and acknowledging that she understood that students were upset about the war. "Miss Brown said that we should not be slouches, and we should continue to shine our oxford shoes and wear a belt with our uniforms. I distinctly recall how indignant we all were. She seemed so oblivious to the dire quality of that time."

Politics held the school's interest but in a manner typical to Garrison Forest. Shelia Love '74 commented on the campus's overwhelming support for Nixon during the 1972 Nixon vs. Humphrey election. "I was a born Democrat who was surrounded by Republicans at school," she recalled. "There was a real intensity with the Nixon buttons and stickers on notebooks, but it was never talked about. It was bad manners to discuss politics and money."

On the evening of January 15, 1973, after lights out, the senior boarders began knocking on dormitory room doors to proclaim that President Nixon had just ordered a cease-fire following peace talks. (The Vietnam War would continue for another two years.) "The seniors were more active, more anti-war," Betsy Searle '74 remembered. "They cried, 'Get up! Get up! The war's over!' and gathered everyone on campus." The group walked in their pajamas up to Lochinvar where Mr. and Mrs. Hlavacek met them on the porch. He offered a few words about the occasion, and Betsy, who joined the board in 1985 and served as president from 1994-99, recalled that some of the seniors were in tears. The next morning, the entire school community gathered in the Chapel for a moment of silence. Two years later, students watched the Watergate proceedings most afternoons crowded around a television in Manor House.

Snowball fight, 1974.

BUDGETARY WOES

"Changes in weekend policy, church attendance, faculty salary [and] curriculum are being forced upon us by the change in times," Mr. Hlavacek stated to the trustees in February 1970. But making the necessary changes required funds that Garrison Forest simply did not have during the 1970s. Though the school began the decade with a large enrollment of 127 boarders and 171 day scholars, the trustees projected an operating budget deficit of $25,000 by June 1970. The school's unsure financial footing included only $213,000 in endowment and Annual Fund efforts averaging $20,000 per year. The aborted move to Geist Road and merger with St. Timothy's had yielded $1.8 million in gifts and pledges and an additional $530,000 when the Geist Road property was sold in summer 1972. These funds would be used to add new facilities to the Reisterstown Road campus: the Marshall-Offutt academic building, the Charles S. Garland Theater, the F.E. White Middle School, and the Sheridan indoor riding facilities. All the while, the school continued to face constant, budget-eating repairs on its older buildings.

Showing school spirit at an athletic event.

Faculty salaries still lagged behind those of regional and national peer institutions. To recruit and retain younger teachers and to attract those with advanced degrees, Garrison Forest needed competitive salaries. In 1975, to fund $40,000 for merit increases, the board made the difficult decision to raise tuition from $1,500 to $1,725 (day) and $3,800 to $4,200 (boarding). Mr. Hlavacek also introduced another change in faculty policy: a retirement plan for all employees. Prior to 1974, only teachers could participate.

Student enrollment was equally discouraging. "We just limped along," quipped trustee Frederick Whitridge, who joined the board in 1974 and served as

Lorraine Polvinale, Spanish teacher and Middle and Upper School head, was at GFS from 1971 to 2007.

Fashions (and hemlines) have changed over the years, but the seniors' white dresses remain a constant. For one family of Garrison Forest graduates, the dress itself has been the constant. In 1948, Katharine Fisher Jenkins chose to wear her grandmother's white morning dress to receive her GFS diploma. Since then, the circa 1890s dress has been altered numerous times to suit the tastes of each subsequent Garrison Forest graduate in the Fisher family. Those donning Margie Macgill James' white dress include:

Kitty Fisher Jenkins '48
Ellen Rogers Jenkins Bullock '71
Louisa Jenkins Stevenson '73

Julie Fisher Colhoun '51
Julie Colhoun Deford '79 *(pictured above with Fred Whitridge, President of the Board)*
Lilly Deford '06

Genie Fisher Elder '55
Genie Elder Moore '78
Ann Este Fisher Stifel '58
Ann Este Stifel '81

Margie MacNeille '68
Ann MacNeille '72
Gabrielle Fisher '86
Amelia Fisher Colhoun '89

president from 1976-81. "We were facing a loss of boarding students, faculty housing was a disaster, and Meadowood was a termite infestation." During the mid-1970s, both Manor House and Robinswood were deemed unsafe for student housing.

By May 1973, the school's financial outlook was beginning to erode Mr. Hlavacek's enthusiasm and optimism. He addressed the trustees, stating that "for the first time, I am not an eternal optimist. The Garrison Forest spirit is facing a test." Teaching staff was cut in math and English, the decades-long tradition of GFS bus service had to be eliminated, among other cost-cutting measures. Mr. Hlavacek voiced his concern that with costs "already pared to the bone, [budget cuts] must not be permitted to jeopardize the quality of the education offered."

Boarding applications were 20 percent lower than the previous year, and many families cited the school's lack of facilities as a reason for their lack of interest in the school. After peaking in 1970-71 with 137 boarders, enrollment dipped below 100 boarders just four years later. Garrison Forest's campus was far from the only issue. Independent girls' boarding schools around the country were losing students to the several New England male boarding schools that had gone coed. And as day schools around the country added upper grades, many students were choosing to remain at home for their high school years. Then there was the national debate on whether girls' schools were antiquated relics of a gentler time. "There was a lot of the national discussion about whether girls' schools could survive," recalled Liza Musgrave. "We were getting beamed across the board with feminist messages that we needed to go out and change the world. And was this the best environment for that? I felt then and do now that it is."

The school's solution to its eroding enrollment was to hire its first full-time director of admission: Stuart Rinehart Stewart '66. She immediately created an alumnae referral program, and she and Mr. Hlavacek began travelling, particularly in the South. The trustees vowed that if boarding enrollment did not increase, the school would maintain a much smaller boarding program and introduce five-day boarding.

In August 1976, Mr. Hlavacek hired as business manager a young Army officer and West Point graduate who had fought in Vietnam. Charles C. "Butch" Darrell served in that capacity for six years before Agnes "Aggie" C. Underwood, who succeeded Mr. Hlavacek, tapped him to join the Middle School faculty full time as a history teacher. "It was lean times, and there was a lot of doubt that the school was going to survive," recounted Mr. Darrell of his business office days. "[Before I took the job], I remember talking to a

McDonogh parent. When I told him that I was going to be the business manager at Garrison, he said, 'Oh, you're going to take the fall, that school's going to fail.' That was generally the attitude."

The school ran an operating deficit throughout Mr. Hlavacek's tenure and well into Mrs. Underwood's years. "We never once balanced the budget," Mr. Darrell admits. "I came within $7,000 of it one year and felt like I won the Super Bowl. We had a lot of long-term debt, and there were a lot of [families] that just weren't paying tuition. We were fixing [buildings] with wire and duct tape. Larry was very gentle with me. There were a lot of people who would have come down very hard on me, but he was very patient. He understood that I would stay here for a long time, and that there was hope for me."

Mr. Hlavacek's and Mrs. Underwood's instincts proved correct. Mr. Darrell left the business office in 1982 for the Middle School history classroom. In 1978, he was tapped to coach the varsity lacrosse team, and before retiring his GFS coaching whistle in 2005, he coached field hockey, lacrosse, and basketball for the Upper and Middle Schools. To honor his legacy on the GFS playing fields and his kindness, grace, and indomitable spirit in the classroom and throughout the school community, the school's basketball courts in the Elizabeth B. Searle '74 Athletic Center are named for Mr. Darrell.

Charles C. "Butch" Darrell, Middle School history teacher, coach, and former GFS business manager.

Garland Theater play, 1983.

In 1974, the campus gained a new performance and assembly venue with the 401-seat Garland Theater. The building honors Charles S. Garland, who served as board president from 1951-57. Garland Theater hosts numerous school performances annually, including plays, musicals, and dance productions, as well as Morning Meeting for the Upper School.

Mr. Hlavacek in his office.

PLANNING FOR THE FUTURE

To navigate the school's financial and enrollment challenges and to determine its future needs, the trustees appointed the school's first long-range planning committee in 1971. A proponent of the committee, Mr. Hlavacek urged it "…to be flexible, to keep re-examining, to be ready to jump but not impulsively." In May 1975, trustee Frederick Whitridge was named chair of the committee.

Coordinate education and coeducation continued to be topics discussed by the committee, as did five-day boarding, and opening boarding to grades seven and eight. Eliminating the boarding program completely was also on the table. With the school going through re-evaluation and facing a projected operating deficit of $140,000, the long-range planning committee took a bold step. In winter 1976, it re-initiated merger discussions with St. Timothy's. As it had five years earlier, the subject consumed the trustee meeting in April 1976. The board examined proposals to merge with St. Timothy's and not to merge but become solely a day school. Mr. Hlavacek urged a timely decision, noting that "time, money and morale, spirit and the life of the school and its members can only suffer from indecision and absence of guiding policy." Alumnae and student were adamantly against it. "Their alumnae vocally shot it down, and our alumnae vocally shot it down," Mr. Whitridge recalled.

In May 1976, the board, once again, voted to remain Garrison Forest School and continue to be a day/boarding school. This time, however, the vote was much closer than it had been in 1971, with 12 votes in favor of remaining a stand-alone school and seven against. "It was obvious to all of us that now that we were here and going to stay here, we needed to figure out what we needed and in what order," Mr. Whitridge said. Listing facility priorities was not a difficult task. "There probably wasn't a building on campus that didn't need maintenance," he noted.

By 1977, part of planning for the future meant planning for a new head of school. Mr. Hlavacek's tenure began with the promise of a new campus and opportunity to build a new school—a heady prospect for any educational leader. He then faced the challenges of a failed move, a divisive decision not to merge with St. Timothy's, a national recession, and transforming social change. Mrs. Hlavacek reflected on what her late husband brought to his role: "A lot of his legacy was just getting through those years and guiding the school through that decade. He just kept the course in a thoughtful, kind way. We loved the 10 years at Garrison and left with great affection."

Presiding over Commencement.

Garrison Forest's indefinable, yet palpable, school spirit, a quality embraced by the Hlavaceks, was another key factor in weathering the decade. "The school spirit, which was openly manifest even during those tumultuous times, was a joy to behold," said Rev. Hammond. "The behavior of the young women at Garrison Forest School in my time was, for the most part, exemplary. I remember very few disciplinary issues on a day-to-day basis. For those who were academically gifted, the educational opportunities were unlimited. For those who needed perhaps to work a little harder to achieve, the endless extra effort, which all members of the faculty seemed willing to provide, enabled achievement beyond what one normally might expect."

After decades in independent schools and a very long decade leading one, Mr. Hlavacek's next career move offered a refreshing change of pace: Executive Director of the Edward E. Ford Foundation. The school honored Mr. Hlavacek's leadership, Mrs. Hlavacek's unwavering enthusiasm, and their shared love of sport by establishing the Linda and Lawrence H. Hlavacek Athletic Award, which is presented annually on Awards Day.

Lochinvar, the stately castle on the hill in the woods, has been home to GFS heads and their families since 1964 when the school purchased the house from the Xanders family. The home and its nearly 13-acre property, adjacent to campus, includes the remains of a small chapel. Known as Lochinvar since it was built (circa 1915), the house shares its name with the hero in Sir Walter Scott's "Marmion" poem. Its castle-inspired structure with its six towers has welcomed the GFS community for teas, dances, meetings, dinners, Christmas tree decorating and Halloween parties, and barbeques. For years, the school used the adjacent former servants' quarters for faculty housing. In 1999, GFS converted the small clapboard house into a daycare center for faculty and staff.

Students and their Jack-o-Lanterns on the front porch of Lochinvar.

An early photo of some of The Valley School faculty and students in front of the school's converted dairy barn on a former farm in Owings Mills. Far left is Kitty Marshall Washburne '46, Valley School's founding headmistress.

MERGER WITH THE VALLEY SCHOOL

From 1910-48, Garrison Forest had a coeducational primary department, renamed the Infantry in the 1930s, for four-year-old through fourth grade students. By 1948, though, the all-girls' Lower School (then fifth through eighth grades) and Upper School were bursting at the seams. Needing classrooms for older students, GFS closed the Infantry. With this decision, the school became an educational pioneer by creating a formal, separate division for girls in grades fifth through eighth at a time when few schools, private or public, had a separate program to address the academic, social, and personal development needs of the adolescent girl. In fact, the educational and psychological importance of the middle school years would not be recognized regionally and nationally until the early 1970s.

The loss of a well-established preschool and elementary school, though, was a blow to northern Baltimore County, where population grew steadily during the 1950s. The same forces of development and suburban expansion that would shape Garrison Forest's 1968 decision to move its campus deeper into the countryside were creating the urgent need for an additional elementary school in the area. In 1960, a group of local parents and other citizens formed and funded The Valley School, an independent, nondenominational, coed elementary school. The Valley School opened its doors to about 40 students in two levels: first grade and the readiness program, which offered an additional year of

preparation for children who needed it prior to first grade. Eventually known as prefirst in the educational field, the readiness program placed The Valley School on the national vanguard of elementary education. The Valley School was the first—and, at the time, only—elementary school in the area to offer a readiness program, and among the first in the country to do so.

Nestled on a former farm in Owings Mills, The Valley School's classroom building was a converted dairy barn. The school's founding families had strong ties to Garrison Forest, including founding board member and GFS Infantry alumnus Herman Stump and Valley School's first headmistress, Kitty Marshall Washburne '46. GFS headmaster Tad Montgomery served on The Valley School board when his children were students there.

By 1974, The Valley School enrolled 115 boys and girls from the nursery through sixth grade. But like Garrison Forest and many other independent schools across the region and country, The Valley School was struggling financially and with enrollment challenges. Some Valley School students would leave after the preschool program to attend other independent elementary school programs. Also, the country was embroiled in a recession.

In May 1974, the idea of merging with The Valley School was floated during a GFS board meeting and met with great enthusiasm. "[A merger] would round out educational possibilities at Garrison Forest...with little risk from the financial standpoint," reported Mr. Hlavacek to the GFS board. Benefits included developing a feeder for the upper grades, providing more young students for Garrison Forest's burgeoning summer programs, and bringing the school's total enrollment to around 400 students. Perhaps most importantly, there was "...sentimentally, the pleasure of returning to the tradition of a complete Lower School at Garrison Forest."

The GFS board unanimously approved the merger, and in September 1974, Garrison Forest welcomed The Valley School's fifth and sixth graders into their classes with one catch: new male students could not be admitted to the school's existing all-girl's fifth and sixth grades, but were welcome at the preschool level. (A handful of Valley School's older male students who transferred to Garrison Forest were allowed to continue through fifth grade, but by the late 1970s, boys were phased out at the elementary level.) On August 1, 1975, the merger was official, and a month later, about 80 Valley School boys and girls matriculated. "It was a special time," recalled Gwynn MacDonald '83, who was one of the original Valley School students who joined the GFS fifth grade in 1974. "We received a lot more attention from the upper schoolers [because] having little kids at the school was a novelty. We had uniforms for the first time and felt like big girls."

To accommodate its newest students and teachers, Garrison Forest expanded and renovated the former Study Hall, renaming it Arrowsmith Hall in honor of Valley School trustee George H. C. Arrowsmith. By 1981, the Moncrieffe building was renovated and expanded to house the preschool division and its newest class, a three-year-old program, which was added that year.

Valley School headmistress Newell P. Price became head of the GFS Lower and Middle Schools. In 1980, a year before her retirement, she became head of the Lower School, and past trustee Kingsley Black Moore '54 was named Middle School head. "People were excited about the merger," recalled Ann Gray, a nursery teacher at The Valley School who taught the four-year-olds at GFS and served as head of the Preschool from 1981-99. "We had all the specialists at Valley—art, music, and physical education—and GFS offered more space and the opportunity to be with all ages." After the merger, older students began volunteering in the Preschool and Lower School classrooms through the child development course, which was offered from 1980-2009, or through Independent Senior Projects.

Other Valley School teachers who joined the GFS faculty were Rufus Davis (art), Edie Horney (first grade), Judy Snyder (second grade), Susan Weiss (music), and Stan Zolenas (physical education), with several serving the school in other capacities. Dr. Weiss, who received her Ph.D. while at Garrison Forest, became head of the music department from 1977 until her retirement in 1994. Mrs. Horney also served as GFS director of residential life and later dean of students for the Upper School before returning to her elementary education roots in 1995 as head of the Lower School until her retirement in 2004. With the merger, several Valley School trustees joined the GFS Board, including Valley School board president Peyton "Skippy" S. Cochran, Jr., an Infantry alumnus, past Valley School board president William C. Trimble Jr., and Sally Robinson. Mr. Cochran went on to serve as president of the GFS board from 1982-85; in 1999, he was named trustee Emeritus.

As predicted by Baltimore County planners in the 1960s and '70s, the region exploded, and in 1999, Garrison Forest's Preschool doubled its enrollment. After a complete renovation and expansion of the Lower School building in 1998, Lower School enrollment grew by 50 percent. In 2004, the separate divisions of the Preschool and Lower School were renamed Moncrieffe and Livingston, respectively, and combined to form the Lower Division.

The reintroduction of young students into Garrison Forest brought back several traditions. In the school's earliest years, Miss Livingston mounted a spring play as a means to gather interest in her fledgling school. Performances were also an essential part of Miss Penny's culturally rich Infantry program. Though their purpose is no longer admission-related, Lower Division class plays and the Moncrieffe holiday production continue to be favorites.

Ann Gray, former Valley School teacher and head of the GFS Preschool from 1981-99.

Lower School performance, 1980s.

Thanksgiving feast, 1986.

When head of school Peter O'Neill (left) joined GFS in 1994, he began a seasonal tradition of reading aloud the beloved children's holiday favorite *The Polar Express* to Moncrieffe students, followed by hot chocolate and cookies. Often wearing a bathrobe over his suit, Mr. O'Neill holds the boys' and girls' attention while they, wearing their robes, sit on the floor in Manor House, the site of Garrison Forest's original classrooms.

...Stan Zolenas

Former Valley School faculty who joined GFS: Susan Weiss...

...Rufus Davis

...Edie Horney

Through the 1990s, the children planted donated flower bulbs and a salad garden each spring, traditions reminiscent of the Infantry's "Fairyland" garden.

Art teacher Michele Shepherd (right) and student.

AGNES COCHRAN UNDERWOOD
HEADMISTRESS, 1978-1989

Agnes "Aggie" Cochran Underwood's selection as headmistress was a choice that embraced the school's rich history. Her exuberant spirit, strong character, and sense of humor echoed the personalities of the women who had led the school for its first 50 years, but it would be her keen intellect and drive that would herald a new era for women and girls' education. As the 1970s drew to a close, women were commonplace across numerous career fields and reaching new milestones in the then traditionally male-dominated professions of medicine, law, and business. "The timing was just right to have a female head," noted Elinor Purves McLennan '56. "Aggie was a good leader to show the girls the growing opportunities for women."

Prior to coming to GFS, Mrs. Underwood spent 12 years at The Spence School teaching anthropology, economics, English, history, and social studies before becoming head of Spence's upper school. A Penn Hall School alumna and graduate of Connecticut College and Shady Hill School's graduate program for teaching certification, Mrs. Underwood earned her MBA from Columbia University in 1976. She graduated first in her class and received the prize for the most outstanding contribution to the intellectual life of the school. "There was a lot of excitement about having a woman and her having her MBA," history teacher Judy Reynolds said. "Most school heads did not have that [degree] at that time."

Mrs. Underwood was 36 when she arrived at GFS, but her relative youth was hardly a novelty for the school. Both Miss Marshall and Mr. Montgomery were in their mid-30s when they began their tenures, and at 32 years of age, Miss Offutt was the youngest head of school ever appointed. What was unique, and another harbinger of emerging roles for women, was the fact that Mrs. Underwood was the first woman headmistress with a family—and a very young family at that. Freddy, her only child, was barely a year old when Mrs. Underwood and husband, Fred, arrived in Baltimore. At the time, Fred was on the Columbia University religion faculty. He would commute weekly to Manhattan during his wife's first three years at GFS.

Mrs. Underwood with son Freddy (above) and in her office.

Creative and capricious, witty and widely accomplished, Clinton Arrowood joined the GFS faculty in 1968 as a music appreciation and art history teacher. His talents as a professional illustrator and flutist and his role as founder of the Rococo Company, a Baltimore quartet specializing in Rococo and Baroque music, added immensely to the artistic environment at the school. His delightful drawings of animals and other beings graced GFS T-shirts, yearbooks, posters, and even a wall or two in Meadowood dormitory. He and his friend Don Elliott collaborated on a series of books, including *Of Alligators and Music* and *Frogs and the Ballet*. Mr. Arrowood's playful sense of humor, generous talent, and an even more generous heart made him a favorite of his students and colleagues alike. He died in 1990 while still a member of the GFS faculty.

Little Freddy became a beloved part of the school community. The Pink Minks, a student a cappella 1950s-style doo-wop group, brought young Freddy onto the Garland Theater stage and serenaded him with "Freddy, My Love" from the musical *Grease*. As a toddler, he would visit his mother's office several times a day, and on weekends students babysat at Lochinvar. One particular GFS community member, however, was removed from the childcare list. Mrs. Underwood once asked Clinton Arrowood to watch her son while he was looking after his son Eduardo. The understood plan was that Mr. Arrowood and both boys would be playing in front of Manor House. "I got a call later from the [grocery store] across Reisterstown Road that both boys were at the register, and would I pick them up," Mrs. Underwood chuckled of the incident, which did not mar the deep friendship she shared with the free-spirited Mr. Arrowood.

On Halloween, the boarders created a haunted house at Lochinvar for Freddy and his friends. And when he was old enough to attend Gilman School, his mother, by then a nationally recognized leader, drove carpool in the acknowledged 1980s symbol of suburban motherhood, the station wagon. Most students gave little notice of their headmistress's status as both career woman and mother, but it would be that balance of professional and family life that would define their generation and those to come. During a *Baltimore Sun* interview given in her first few weeks at GFS, she remarked that while "she did not have a baby because [she] wanted to be a role model, [her] life is saying a woman can have a career, be a good mother…and still serve the community."

Mrs. Underwood was acutely aware of her role model status and often spoke with students about careers. Noted Sarah Crosby Schweizer '84, GFS trustee, "It was understood that we were being educated to go out and do whatever we wanted to do." Not coincidentally, the school's first Career Day with alumnae panelists occurred during Mrs. Underwood's first year. Vocational advice was not limited to students. Mrs. Underwood had an interest in faculty development as well. "She was a good mentor to faculty, male and female," recalled Dante Beretta, Ph.D., who began teaching Latin in the Middle School in 1985. "She cared about the careers of her teachers."

Showing the GFS spirit during halftime.

LIGHTING A SPARK

Mrs. Underwood's petite stature and gap-toothed smile belied a seemingly inexhaustible energy and intense focus. "She was a ball of fire," recalled Fred Whitridge. "Alumnae loved her, parents loved her, and she was sharp as a tack." She was also, he noted, out to prove a point. Garrison Forest was facing severe competition for day students, boarding enrollment was dwindling, and the school was struggling financially. "Aggie brought a whole new perspective," he said. Added Elinor McLennan, chuckling, "Aggie was never scared to make a decision. She was a bit of a maverick."

Drawn to Garrison Forest by both the challenges and the school's enduring values, Mrs. Underwood quickly defined the problem. "The issue in the late 1970s was not the school's values but its structure," she said. Garrison Forest's recently formed long-range planning committee had no difficulty prioritizing the structural needs of the campus, but the board and the new headmistress continued to grapple with the questions of the decade. "Should we be a boarding school, a day/boarding school, or go coed?" recalled Mrs. Underwood. "Without a coherent definition of who we were, the school couldn't compete."

When her husband returned to Baltimore each Thursday night, Mrs. Underwood would meet him at Baltimore's Pennsylvania Station. "Freddy was young, I was young, and as you can imagine, I was very tired," she recalled. "One night while waiting at the station, I thought, 'Well, I'll just lie on a bench and put my New York Times over my body.'" She dozed off until someone came up and peeled back a corner of the paper near her head. It was Fred Whitridge, GFS trustee. "He said, 'What are you doing here like some vagrant?'"

Mrs. Underwood with typical teaching accessories during her early years at GFS: son Freddy and a can of diet soda. Though Freddy moved on to the Gilman classrooms, his mother's diet soda habit remained throughout her GFS tenure.

Mrs. Underwood, Elinor Purves McLennan '56, president of the board (top right), and library campaign co-chairs James Riepe and Beaumont Russell Martin '65 break ground for the new Library (pictured below). Prior to its construction, the school's library was housed over the years in Manor House, Moncrieffe, Study Hall, and the basement of Meadowood.

Mrs. Underwood and the trustees set out to create the school's first strategic plan and campus master plan. "Those two pieces put together a structure to position GFS to prosper in a competitive market, ever mindful of its core values," she said. During her first six years, the number of boarding students almost doubled, and day enrollment grew steadily across each of the four divisions. Mrs. Underwood pushed the school's national reputation further with her appointments on high-profile national boards; she served as chairman of the National Association of Independent Schools Council on Boarding Schools, president of the Headmistress' Association of the East, trustee of the Board for Independent Educational Services, and trustee of the National Association of Girls' Boarding Schools (one of the founding groups of the National Coalition of Girls' Schools).

With a master plan in place, the board began a capital campaign. They methodically addressed long-postponed building maintenance issues, renovating and adding key campus improvements. In 1981, the Moncrieffe building was renovated and expanded to house the Preschool. Six years later, the new Library, which was named in 1997 for Elinor Purves McLennan '56, was constructed. The parking lots and road that once separated Meadowood and Marshall-Offutt were replaced to create pedestrian walkways and Penniman Park, in memory of past board president Nicholas G. Penniman III. In 1987, the Frederick W. Whitridge Athletic Pavilion was constructed beside the new tennis courts and named for Mr. Whitridge, an honor the school community managed to keep secret from him until the building's opening celebration. At the time, it was the school's newest athletic facility in over five decades.

Mrs. Underwood's vision and drive were not lost on the students. Leigh McDonald Hall '81 recalled that when she entered GFS in 1975, "it was very relaxed, but when I graduated, the school was changing and the whole atmosphere was becoming more structured." Said Gwynn MacDonald '83, "By Mrs. Underwood's example, we learned that success was something you want, that it's about living up to your potential." As a student in Mrs. Underwood's senior economics class, Gwynn also learned lessons well beyond supply and demand. "Her stories of Columbia made us feel that we could go out in the world and achieve as women," she said. "It wasn't just her career, but the way she managed her career. We learned that you didn't have to be all nails to get ahead. You could have a sense of humor. She was all business while still having charm, character, and humanity."

Part of her charm was evident during Prayers when Mrs. Underwood perched on a high wooden stool, fumbling for reading glasses in the pocket of her trench coat. Glasses found, she read aloud from one of her personal favorites: Louis Sachar's *Sideways Stories from Wayside School*. "Some people wanted her to read something more intellectual, but she was just trying to put some heart into it," chuckled Ann Teaff, whom Mrs. Underwood hired in 1980 as a history teacher before appointing her head of the Upper School in 1988. "Aggie brought a kind of sophistication and seriousness of purpose while keeping it light and fun," remarked Edie Horney.

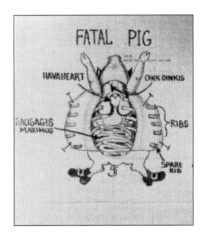

Science teacher Lodie Earll and student dissect a fetal pig, a biology class rite of passage that Mr. Arrowood poked fun at with his "Fatal Pig" drawing (top right).

French teachers Madame Francoise von Mayer (middle) and Madame Micheline Johnson (below). Madame von Mayer taught from 1979-99, and Madame Johnson taught from 1972-97.

RAISING STANDARDS AND EXPECTATIONS

It was Garrison Forest's academic program, however, that experienced the most sweeping change during Mrs. Underwood's 11-year tenure. She continued to build a strong faculty and added key administrative positions, including hiring Kathleen "Kiki" Johnson as the first head of the Upper School and assistant headmistress. The school carefully reviewed curriculum and requirements and added a number of new electives. With a Cleveland H. Dodge Foundation grant in 1983—one of the first awards given to study women and mathematics—GFS used the funds to tighten expectations for all GFS students to go further in math. "There was a kind of electricity that Aggie generated," recalled Joan Smith, dean of students during Mrs. Underwood's tenure. "It was a feeling that we were moving and were on the cusp of making things happen."

B.J. McElderry, art department chair, joined the GFS faculty in 1976.

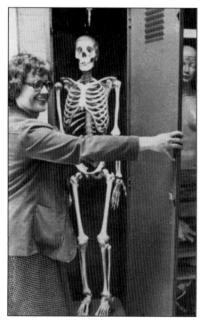

Winifred McDowell taught science for 41 years from 1960 until her retirement in 2001. Her environmental advocacy— and unwavering enthusiasm and kindness— helped to inspire a student-led recycling program in the late 1980s.

Emblematic of the increased rigor was the growing number of Advanced Placement (AP) course offerings. In 1977, Garrison Forest offered six AP courses. By 1983, the number more than doubled. Upper School course offerings increased, with Mrs. Underwood herself teaching economics and anthropology and the occasional seventh grade history course. The Middle School adopted a Latin requirement, and in 1979, the Lower School added a full-time science teacher. Computers, no longer a behemoth on the Manor House sun porch, slowly made their way into classrooms. The new library had a computer lab with MacIntosh computers, and as Susanna Brennan Buchta '84 recalled, "one giant word processor with discs the size of a record album." Equally innovative was the infusion of experiential learning. "In the 1980s, we were doing more project-based learning, which is at the heart of how girls learn best. It was leading edge at the time," Ms. Teaff remarked.

At times, what was happening in the world overshadowed what was being taught in the classroom. Television sets were no longer relegated to the dormitories but were in academic buildings as well. With world and national events of importance, the Upper School teachers would roll a television cart, complete with a "rabbit ear" antenna, into the lobby of Marshall-Offutt. Upper and Middle School students recalled crowding around small TV sets to watch a shuttle launch and the aftermath of the assassination attempt on President Ronald Reagan. When the Challenger space shuttle exploded on January 28, 1986, students watched the events unfold on TV and were given the choice to attend or not attend their afternoon classes. "We told the girls that this was more important than anything we could teach," said Mrs. Smith.

College placement was a critical part of raising the academic profile, and Mrs. Underwood's expectation was that every girl would apply to and enroll in college. Garrison Forest's college placement track record had been strong since the school's founding when both members of the first graduating class passed the challenging Bryn Mawr College entrance exam. Prior to Mrs. Underwood's tenure, though, college counseling had been handled part time by an Upper School faculty member or administrator. In 1984, Mrs. Underwood created the school's first full-time college counselor position and hired history teacher Joan Mudge to fill it. "Aggie told me my goal should be that every girl go to a four-year college and not a two-year," said Mrs. Mudge. "The new focus was a good thing," agreed French teacher Micheline Johnson. "It gave all students a lift that special care was being taken for all students."

At the same time, Garrison Forest dropped the student ranking from the college profile. "We were one of the first independent schools to question colleges about the impact it would make if we dropped ranking," said Mrs. Mudge, who served as college counselor until her retirement in 2007. "Today I don't know of any independent schools that rank."

Equally critical to raising the academic bar was increasing diversity among the school community. The number of students of color had increased since 1967, when the first African-American students enrolled, but the school was far from where it wanted to be. At the beginning of the 1980s, minority enrollment stood at six percent. "We had one person of color [in my class] and I was the only Jew," Gwynn remarked. "All the hymns we sang during Vespers and Prayers were Episcopal. I was raised Jewish and taught that you know yourself better if you know the rest of the world. I felt as if we were the enlightened end of the old world. You could still feel and touch 'old' Garrison, yet there was room for others and me. The attitude, I felt, had changed."

During her interview, Ms. Teaff recalled asking Mrs. Underwood about the number of students of color. "Aggie replied, 'Don't judge by where we

Students have enjoyed faculty-led international study trips to such locales as Spain, Russia, France, and England since the 1970s. They are typically held during spring break or summer, and the number of countries visited has expanded since 1995 to include Greece, Peru, Japan, China, and the Czech Republic. Beginning in the mid-1980s, Ann Teaff (pictured fourth from right), then history department chairman, led Cold War-era school trips to Europe and Russia. "Ronald Reagan had declared the Soviet Union the 'Evil Empire,' and we were in the throes of containment," Ms. Teaff said of the three trips she led to Russia. "The idea of the trips was to connect to the people and culture to help overcome political prejudices." In 1986, Ms. Teaff launched the school's Modern Russian History course, one of the only such Russian history electives at the time among independent schools. She became head of the Upper School in 1988, a post she held until she left GFS a decade later.

In the 1980s, the Upper School introduced QUEST—experiential overnight class trips to campgrounds, outdoor leadership ropes courses, and sometimes cities—for group bonding and to further class unity.

In 1982, the Lower School introduced its Uninterrupted Silent Sustained Reading (USSR) program to promote reading. The program was renamed Drop Everything and Read (DEAR) in the 1990s.

are now. Think about coming on the team and helping us take GFS to a new place.' " The board and faculty were engaged in nearly constant conversations about strategies to increase the number of people of color among students, teachers, administrators, and board members. "I remember meetings at Lochinvar discussing ways to effectively bring in more racially diverse students by giving them support and by helping the rest of the community to understand difference," said Mrs. Mudge, who, as part of her graduate work in the mid-1980s, conducted a support group for African-American students. As a result of that group, the students established the Cultural Awareness Club. "The students did not feel the school was ready yet for a Black Awareness or Black Student Union," she noted. The latter would be founded by GFS students nearly a decade later.

In the early 1980s, the newly formed Baltimore Educational Scholarship Trust (BEST) and the introduction of tuition loan programs helped increase the school's diversity. Throughout the course of the decade, the Owings Mills corridor's diversity increased as the suburban center anticipated by county planners in the 1960s came to fruition. The school focused on outreach to students of color and Jewish children, a strategy not without critics, Mrs. Underwood recalled. "Baltimore was very Southern, and there was pushback, but the trustees did the right thing to strategically spend money to renovate and add teachers," she said. By 1988-89, students of color represented 15 percent of the student body, and by 2008-09, the percentage had risen to 25 percent.

FINDING
FINANCIAL FOOTING

The deficit budgets of the 1970s continued to plague the school throughout Mrs. Underwood's tenure. Enrollment was rising, but so were the costs of implementing new programs, increasing faculty salaries and student scholarships, and continuing to handle the maintenance on the older buildings. "We were living hand-to-mouth on each tuition dollar and had no endowment to speak of," noted Betsy Searle '74. And there was still the old mystique of getting by on sheer charm, as had often been the case during Miss Marshall's and Miss Offutt's era. "In the [GFS] community, there was a delicate balance of how we acknowledged finances," said Joan Smith. "There was still bitterness about the [aborted] move [to Geist Road], and at the time, tuition was a fraction of what it cost to attend the school."

That began to change in 1980, when the school initiated a capital campaign to raise money for endowment, a new library, Moncrieffe renovations for the Preschool, and to create more dormitory rooms by moving the infirmary out of Shriver. In 1984, another petite, tenacious woman joined the GFS administration, and her mark on fundraising would change the school's financial footing. Molly Mundy Hathaway '61 became director of special gifts in 1984. "I am not certain if I hired Molly," quipped Mrs. Underwood. "Molly saw a need and hired herself." (Actually, parent James Riepe recommended Molly for the job.) Two years later, she was promoted to director of development and orchestrated the largest fundraising growth in the school's history. When Molly retired in 1999, the endowment stood at $19.8 million, annual giving was just below the $1 million year mark, the campus had been entirely renovated and updated, and alumnae were supporting their alma mater as never before.

One of the school's biggest assets was its Reisterstown Road frontage. In 1976, the board had made what was a highly controversial decision to sell several acres for commercial purposes, though it would be another decade-plus before any property was actually sold. "We were told that the community would never support it," Elinor McLennan said. "We had a town meeting in the gym and got some tough questions, but we didn't have any place else to get the money we needed." Eventually, in 1989, R&H Motors bought 2.5 acres from the school. The trustees approved $1 million of the $1.6 million in net proceeds for endowment, with the balance for building maintenance and renovation.

Mrs. Underwood shared another quality with previous headmistresses: She, too, adored dogs. "Teatsie," her Norwich Terrier and later, "Goldie," a Jack Russell, were as ubiquitous as her cans of diet cola. Ironically, it was during Mrs. Underwood's tenure that the school's nearly eight decades of free-roaming campus canines came to a close. Since the days of Miss Livingston, the campus often resembled a pound, if not a zoo. From the well-behaved German Shepherds of history teacher Miss Hall and French teacher Miss Boyd to Miss Offutt's Cocker Spaniels who would fight loudly with other dogs outside her classroom window, faculty and staff members' dogs had the run of campus. Mr. Hlavacek's Basset hound, Shamus, was an expert at sniffing out food and sharing his copious slobber with the owner of the desired snack. Mr. Arrowood was known to place Galatea, his pet frog and muse, under his hat, which he would tip to surprised students. By 1975, off-campus faculty and staff were not permitted to bring dogs onto campus, a rule dog-lover Mrs. Underwood relaxed. By 1990, due to health and safety concerns, dogs were no longer permitted in academic buildings, nor could the owner bring an animal to school during the day.

Mrs. Underwood's era coincided with the end of an era at GFS, when in 1989, head of housekeeping Irene Jackson retired. For 40 years, she lent her formidable sense of style, beauty, and decorum to Robinswood dormitory and to the rest of the campus, even tending to the geese on the pond. Petite and elegant, she oversaw campus special events and added charm to the campus by arranging fresh flowers for the buildings, hosting occasional teas for the preschoolers, and celebrating the birthdays of her Robinswood charges with cake in her apartment. (In the early 1980s, Robinswood was renovated as faculty residences.) Winifred McDowell recalled that once, when Miss Jackson, who was well-loved by students, faculty, and staff alike, caught a student "baking" refrigerated cookie dough by ironing the cookies—the kitchen was off-limits to the students—Miss Jackson's sweet demeanor was not so sweet.

In spring 1989, Mrs. Underwood announced her resignation to become head of the National Cathedral School for Girls. The endowment stood at $3.6 million, enrollment was steady, and the school's academic program was on the map regionally and nationally. "When she arrived Aggie loved Garrison Forest, but she wanted it to change, to be the best it could be and be the best for its students," Ms. Teaff reflected. "She turned out to be visionary."

The elegant and stately Robinswood, ancestral home of founding director of the GFS riding program, Suzanne White Whitman, was purchased by the school in 1945. It was used as a student dormitory until the early 1980s, when it was renovated as faculty residences.

SPIRITED COMPETITION

The faces of Garrison Forest's spirit.

I'm the Garrison Spirit

Garrison Forest's storied athletic history began quite humbly with one sport in 1915: a basketball team that practiced and played on an outdoor court in the winter. Their sparse athletic schedule included games against GFS faculty. Their uniforms—at the time, the only required school uniforms—consisted of stiff cotton sailor tops and voluminous bloomers falling just below stocking-clad knees (above). Fifteen years later, field hockey coach Miss Marshall ditched the black stockings and allowed her athletes to play bare-legged, causing somewhat of a stir among local girls' school opponents. Since that first GFS team, the school has fielded numerous divisional and national championship teams across an array of sports. In its centennial year, Garrison Forest's athletic program fielded 13 sports with 42 teams, including nationally recognized riding and polo programs and dance.

Sarah LeBrun Ingram '84 (below), GFS trustee, played golf while at GFS but not for a school team. Garrison Forest did not introduce golf as an interscholastic sport until 2007. Sarah became one of the sport's top-ranked amateur golfers, winning eight U.S. Opens and three U.S. Women's Mid-Amateur crowns.

While a GFS student, Beth Botsford '99, who at the time was a member of the North Baltimore Aquatic Club, won two gold medals in the 1996 Summer Olympics: one in the individual 100-meter backstroke; and another as a member of the women's relay team in the 400-meter medley. During Beth's Olympic heyday, Mr. O'Neill often introduced her as "the only member of the GFS swim team." In 2006, the school added swimming as a physical education option, making use of nearby McDonogh School's pool.

In fall 1977, the varsity lacrosse team became the first GFS team to travel abroad for athletic competition and cultural expansion. Their trip "across the pond" included games in England and Scotland and enthusiastic coaching by head coach Butch Darrell (bottom right), who inspired the team with his motto: "Play Hard, Play Fair, and Have Fun." Middle School physical education teacher and coach Karen Mallonee (top right) also accompanied the team. Note the team sweatshirts with "USA" spelled out in tape.

MASCOTS

Garrison Forest's teams had no official mascot until 1982 when Forum voted to name the unicorn the GFS mascot, a selection that would be short-lived. A few years earlier, music and art history teacher Clinton Arrowood drew an alligator playing lacrosse as a nod to the then preppy clothing fashion craze, but the alligator was not the mascot.

BAMBI

In the 1930s and '40s, Bambi, a donkey, served as the unofficial GFS mascot. The donkey would ride in the back of a station wagon to graze on the sidelines of a field hockey game. If Garrison Forest had home field advantage, Bambi might be led to campus from a nearby farm. Bambi had a leading role in another campus tradition: "The Road," the Christmas pageant penned by Miss Offutt and performed by the seventh grade during the school day in the Chapel. Bambi was to be led by Joseph and carry the student playing Mary through the woods and into the Chapel. The reality of the ride was far from divine. With Bambi both reticent and rambunctious, Mary had to hold on for dear life while Bambi—and the subsequent donkeys who assumed the role after Bambi's demise—clomped through the woods. By the late 1980s, the venue had changed to Garland Theater, but a live donkey still continued in the cast for a few years. "The Road" was performed through the late 1990s before the tradition ceased.

DRIBBLES

Dribbles, a stuffed monkey, made its appearance in 1954 as a good-luck charm for the varsity basketball team. Over the years, the monkey appropriated a blue tunic, which was signed on the inside by team captains in lacrosse and field hockey. In 2006, an aging Dribbles retired to the GFS Archives, and the varsity hockey team introduced Dribbles II, another stuffed monkey, to carry on the tradition. In a GFS team uniform and with a miniature hockey stick, Dribbles II attends each varsity hockey game.

VICTORIA

The basketball team acquired another mascot in 1954 with the arrival of Victoria, a blond-haired, pink-cheeked doll purchased at the St. Thomas' bazaar. According to *The Blueprint*, Victoria was given to Sallie Hurst Worthington '56 for Christmas. Sallie created a blue sweater and "sturdy browns" (oxford shoes required of all Garrison girls) for the doll. Victoria was adopted by the cheerleading squad, which had been founded by students in 1947. Wearing white sweaters over their blue dress uniforms, cheerleaders could be found on the GFS sidelines from the late 1940s through the mid-1970s.

THE UNICORN

From 1982-85, the unicorn was the mascot, a selection inspired by an event in 1979 when Mr. Arrowood enlisted then business manager and varsity hockey coach Butch Darrell to raffle off a unicorn hunt for a school auction. The plan was simple: Mr. Arrowood would play his flute while the auction winners would enjoy a picnic lunch in the woods near the Chapel. Mr. Darrell, in a makeshift unicorn costume, would appear behind a tree in the distance and disappear. Instead, when the students caught a glimpse of Mr. Darrell, they yelled, "Let's get him!" After falling in a ditch and ripping his pants, Mr. Darrell managed to get to his office in Manor House and shove his costume under his desk. Two minutes later, the four girls ran in his office. "You were the unicorn," they shouted. "I certainly was not," he replied. Then they pointed at the grass stains on his pants. "Oh, yes, you were."

THE GRIZZLY

In 1985, a student contest resulted in a new mascot: the Garrison Forest Grizzly. A beloved symbol at the school—and fitting for an institution with the word "forest" in its name—the Grizzly has bared its claws when necessary through depictions of the paw print on sports gear to show opposing teams the "Paw Power" of Garrison Forest. The Grizzly made its first appearance as a mascot costume in 1986 (right) and has had several different costumes since.

RIDING

A riding program existed during the school's first two decades, but it was not until 1931 and Suzanne White Whitman (see below) that the program advanced to a new level. She recruited students who rode at Garrison Forest, dramatically improving the quality of the riding program and creating a national boarding school. In 1933, students founded the Riding Club with strict admissions tests and an annual spring horse show.

POLO

Polo was a male-dominated sport when Garrison Forest launched the first all-girls high school team in the United States in 1979. At the urging of Julie Colhoun Deford '79, her parents Dan and Julie Fisher Colhoun '51 founded the GFS polo program. Mr. Colhoun served as the team's first coach, and daughters Julie, Martha Colhoun Williams '85, and granddaughter Lilly Deford '06 played for GFS. The team and its players are consistently ranked among the top in the country.

SUZANNE WHITE WHITMAN

In 1931, Mrs. Whitman, or "Miss Whit" as her students called her, founded the official riding program. With grace, charm, and tenacity, she created and led an exceptional department that put Garrison Forest on the map as one of the top riding programs in the country, a reputation still held today. "She was the unquestioned queen of the barn," noted Carrington Dame Hooper '54. "She was strict, knew what she was doing, and she loved to ride fast side-saddle in all her majesty." Fittingly, Mrs. Whitman retired in 1960, the same year as Miss Marshall and Miss Offutt.

ETHEL HOFFMAN

Ethel Hoffman '38 was an equally unforgettable and inspirational figure in the formative years of the riding program. Cheerful and diplomatic, gentle and generous, she brought out the best in her students. And as an accomplished equestrian who cut an elegant figure astride a horse, she offered the best as an example. Recruited in 1941 by Mrs. Whitman, Ethel taught riding at GFS and served as director of riding from 1960-63 until her tragic death in December 1963, when she was struck by a hit-and-run driver in front of the school. The February 1964 *Blueprint* included these words in memoriam: "She combined a marvelous sense of humor and lightness of touch to a perfect degree of seriousness and practicality to do for others what very few would do again in their lives." After her death, her sister Kitty McLane Hoffman '37 assumed Ethel's teaching duties and directed the riding department for nine years alongside friend Maud Barker Jones '34, who was one of the founders of the GFS Riding Club. In addition to teaching riding, Maud also directed many GFS dramatic productions.

BASKETBALL

Basketball was the earliest sport offered at Garrison Forest, and for decades, "the thing," as proclaimed in school yearbooks.

FIELD HOCKEY

Miss Marshall introduced this sport to GFS when she joined the staff in 1928 as coach and athletic director. She coached the basketball and hockey teams prior to and well into her tenure as co-headmistress.

BADMINTON

The badminton team, founded and coached by French teacher Miss Boyd, became a GFS sport in 1945.

CROSS COUNTRY

Garrison Forest added cross country in 1993.

LACROSSE

The first mention of a lacrosse team was in the 1932 yearbook, but it would not be until 1961 when the school fielded another lacrosse team.

SOCCER

Soccer was added to the athletic roster of teams in 1975.

SOFTBALL

This sport became part of the school's sports offerings in 1975 as well.

TENNIS

Tennis was first offered circa 1920 as a club sport. The first interscholastic squad was created in 1936.

GARRISON FOREST SCHOOL

75
SPIRITED
YEARS

1910-1985

ALEXANDER A. UHLE
INTERIM HEAD OF SCHOOL, 1989-1990

Hired for one year as interim head, Alexander "Alex" Uhle, the former Foxcroft and Greenwich Academy headmaster, served Garrison Forest at a critical time. "The role of interim head, arguably, is to keep the ship on course with a steady hand at the helm," he told *The Blueprint* in March 1990. With his seasoned eye and no-nonsense approach, he immediately focused on the business of running Garrison Forest. The campus also benefited from the professional experience of his wife Sally, a former independent school business manager, in her informal role on campus.

His seasoned guidance included boosting faculty and staff salary short-falls by $160,000 and working closely with the school's new business manager, Bill Hodgetts, and the trustees to continue the master plan adopted during Mrs. Underwood's tenure by remodeling Robinswood and doing upkeep on Meadowood, Shriver, and Senior House. Mr. Uhle's lasting impact, though, was on the operating budget. For most of the 1980s, GFS ran deficit budgets. "Things really started to click," noted Mr. Hodgetts. "Alex came in and had an eye for it, and there was great synergy to the board. Aggie raised the academic profile. Now we had to get our financial house in order."

Shortly thereafter, the school balanced its budget and embarked on a $12 million campaign for endowment and a fine and performing arts center. Mr. Uhle's crystal ball-gazing for what the campus could be proved to be crystal clear. "Why not prefer to dream, per chance to build, a new structure on the location of the old gym, which would provide for enhanced community dining, and for new and much needed space for art and music and sometime later a new gym?" he urged the board. In 1996, the Fine and Performing Arts Center, later named for Molly Mundy Hathaway '61, opened its doors, followed in 2002 by the Campus Center, and the Elizabeth B. Searle '74 Athletic Center—all on the exact locations Mr. Uhle had suggested.

Mr. Uhle and wife Sally.

Garrison Forest has marked its anniversaries. Pictured here is the 75th celebration in 1985.

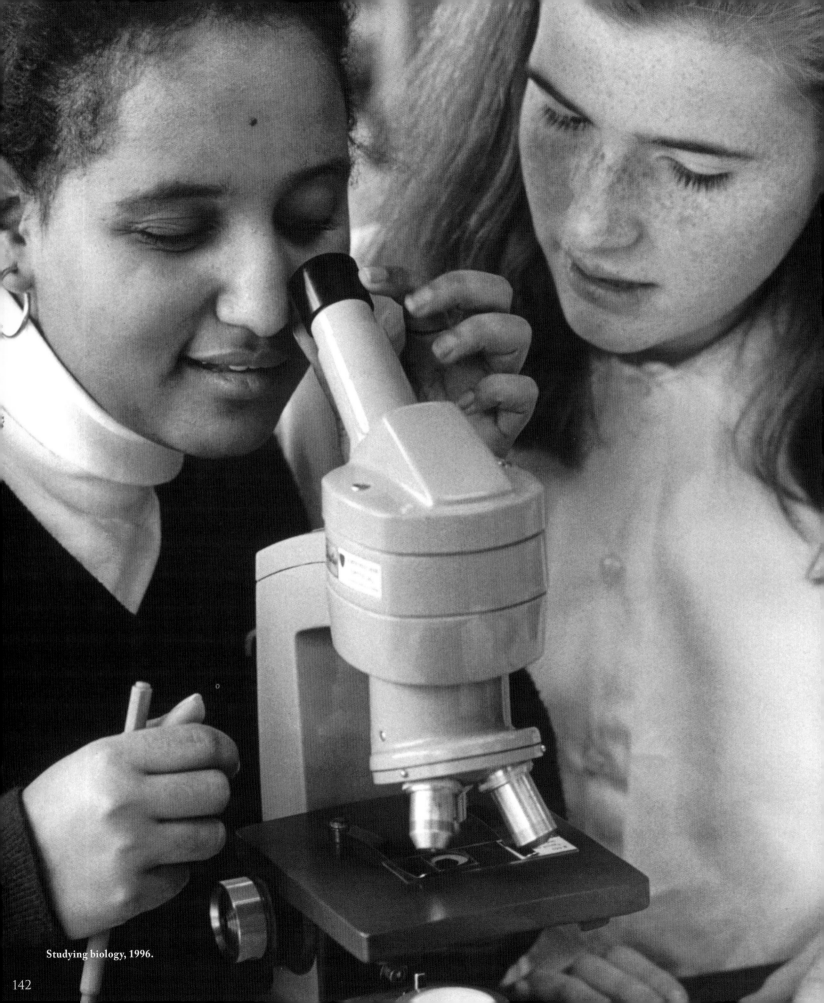

Studying biology, 1996.

ELSA M. BOWMAN
HEADMISTRESS, 1990-1994

In 1990, the school was 80 years old and a very different place from the days of Miss Livingston. Every Garrison Forest School graduate was attending a four-year college with the expectation that a fulfilling career would follow. In fact, by 1990, over half of the U.S. workforce was female, and women were succeeding in every conceivable career field, including the military where more than 40,000 women deployed for Operation Desert Shield/Desert Storm in the Persian Gulf War. Technology and the dawn of the Information Age were changing—and shrinking—the world. The fact that 1990 marked the beginning of the last decade of the 20th century did not go unnoticed. "We were already anticipating the 21st century, both the promise and the fright of it," remembered Ann Teaff.

It was an auspicious time indeed for Elsa "Midge" M. Bowman to begin her tenure as headmistress. A teacher and administrator for 30 years, Mrs. Bowman graduated magna cum laude from Pomona with a bachelor's in music and philosophy before heading East to get her master's from Yale. A native of Seattle, she returned to the West Coast to begin her career in education. Prior to joining Garrison Forest School, Mrs. Bowman had been headmistress of Westridge School for Girls in Pasadena, California.

Reserved and thoughtful, quick-witted and well-read, she was both an intellect and an artist. A member of Phi Beta Kappa and an eloquent speaker and writer, she was also a gifted pianist. Mrs. Bowman and husband David, a retired executive from Lockheed Corporation and an accomplished musician as well, moved to Maryland with two baby grand pianos. Both instruments found a home in the front room of Lochinvar. During school gatherings, the Bowmans, who had two grown children, Megan and Matthew, often would perform duets for faculty, alumnae, and other guests. When trustees dined at Lochinvar, the Bowmans chose medleys of George Gershwin and Jerome Kern, among others. Mrs. Bowman also used her Lochinvar "conservatory" to rehearse chamber music with some of the students. And while a fan of Maryland's changing seasons, she learned quickly how brutal the humidity could be. "Without air-conditioning, the

Mrs. Bowman.

Matthew, Midge, David, and Megan
Bowman.

Enjoying the Thanksgiving feast with
preschoolers.

ivories started to come off the piano keys and we had to get a dehumidifier for the living room," she recalled.

Another passion was the field of human development. Mrs. Bowman had conducted doctoral-level research in human development at the Fielding Institute and at the Antioch University Institute for the Study of Adult Development. A product of a girls' school herself, Mrs. Bowman was well versed in the then-emerging research on the importance of adolescence in girls' development and the key role girls' schools can play in fostering self-esteem. As researchers such as Harvard professor Carol Gilligan made national headlines with information on women's development and the critical loss of self-confidence in girls during adolescence, Mrs. Bowman shared the emerging research with faculty, parents, and alumnae and the importance of the single-sex educational environment for girls.

Mrs. Bowman's writings on single-sex education appeared in several national publications. In *USA Today* in October 1991, she challenged the National Organization of Women Legal Defense and Educational Fund and American Civil Liberties Union's suits to open Detroit's all-boy academies to girls. She advocated that they support the Detroit Board of Education's plans to open an all-girls' academy: "As the head of an independent all-girl school, I know that girls thrive in a single-sex educational environment which provides high academic expectations, strong gender role models and leadership training—all of which counteract the negative stereotyping still prevalent in our society."

A nationally recognized leader among girls' schools, Mrs. Bowman had helped to found the National Coalition of Girls' Schools (NCGS) in 1991. NCGS was created through the merger of the Coalition of Girls' Boarding Schools and the Coalition of Girls' Day Schools, at a time, ironically, when most of the girls' boarding schools were led by men. When Mrs. Bowman assumed the NCGS presidency in 1993, she became part of a larger GFS legacy with the organization. While at Garrison Forest, Mrs. Underwood had helped to found the National Coalition of Girls' Boarding Schools. "Aggie brought vision, chutzpah, and an unwillingness to concede that girls' schools were no longer relevant," explained Whitney Ransome, co-executive director of NCGS before joining GFS in 2008 as director of the James Center. "When girls' schools were launched in the 1800s, it was a revolutionary movement. I view NCGS as a second revolution. We needed to update everyone's opinion of what a girls' school looked like. Midge, too, had a fire in her belly about raising the profile of girls' schools. She was a gracious, collaborative leader and a class act."

At Garrison Forest, Mrs. Bowman tapped a rich vein for research in women's development: the alumnae. She surveyed them on the seasons of a woman's life and on the complex relationship between mothers and daughters, the results of which were shared in popular speeches and *Alumnae Magazine* articles. "The alumnae responses were humbling in their honesty and trust of me," Mrs. Bowman recalled. "I felt like 'Dear Abby,' and I think I created bonds between the alumnae and me that were unique." She often shared her findings with students. For her second year at GFS, she adopted the theme of women's leadership, and many of her speeches spoke of her admiration for the school as a "leadership training ground." A year later, a new student leadership program created by Ms. Teaff hosted 60-plus student leaders at a retreat.

GOING GREEN

Having lived in Southern California, Mrs. Bowman immediately embraced the green of Garrison Forest. "After the concrete and asphalt of Los Angeles, this area seems like a little piece of paradise," she wrote to GFS parents in summer 1990. She enjoyed walks back and forth from Lochinvar, often drawing inspiration from nature for her carefully crafted remarks to the school community.

Her first year coincided with the "greening" of the campus and the beginning of a healthier era. Led by the Environmental Support Group student organization, recycling efforts began in 1989, with collection boxes for aluminum cans placed in each campus building. By1990, GFS phased out of what had been a tradition at Garrison Forest and at many

Earth Day celebrations in the early 1990s included stream and forest clean-up efforts by students. The school's first environmental efforts began in 1970 with the first Earth Day and school activities organized by science teacher Kathleen Gran and several students.

Honoring Mrs. Bowman's Scottish
heritage, a bagpiper leads the Lower
School to Mrs. Bowman's inauguration,
at which the students presented her
with a GFS pillow.

independent schools across the country: smoking on campus. After 80 years, students could no longer smoke at school and adults could only smoke in private, on-campus residences. Gone were the days of seniors being invited to share an after-dinner smoke with faculty in the Manor House sitting rooms, of Mr. Elliott teaching a class with a smoldering Viceroy in his hand, and of "The Pit," the latter-day student smokers' outdoor area.

CELEBRATIONS AND CHALLENGES

For the first time in Garrison Forest's history, the school planned an elaborate installation celebration for its new headmistress. On October 19 and 20, 1990, Mrs. Bowman was installed during three separate events: one with the Preschool, another with the Lower and Middle Schools, and a final with the Upper School and alumnae, trustee, and parent guests, replete with academic regalia. In her installation speech, she embraced the ideals of the school's founding and their role in the new decade and coming century: "The philosophy and the objectives of the school have evolved and changed over the past 80 years, but the essence of our mission has remained true: to instill in our students a love of learning, a strong sense of self-worth, and a commitment to the welfare of others."

Amidst the pomp and circumstance, however, were ongoing challenges. Once again, the country was facing an economic downturn, and national boarding schools were experiencing a dip in enrollment. In fact, Garrison Forest's boarding population had declined for each of the preceeding three years. In fall of 1990, the board unanimously approved an eighth-grade boarding program as a means of bolstering the school's residential population. Though the endowment had reached $4.2 million and the board was scrutinizing every area of the budget, the school was still struggling to run in the black. The buzzword for the new decade was "downsizing," yet the school needed to grow to stay competitive. More financial aid was needed, and even with Mr. Uhle's distribution of $160,000 for faculty salaries the year before, compensation still lagged behind regional norms. And while the school supported a handful of computer labs and a strong computer program—by 1990, computer instruction was offered from kindergarten to twelfth grade—staying up to date with technology demanded significant resources.

During her first faculty meeting, Mrs. Bowman minced no words in addressing the school's financial footing. "For all our idealism, we must be a business," she said. "This year, as in the past, we are operating at a substantial deficit. This is unacceptable to me. While we work to increase enrollment as the ultimate answer to our budget problem, [we] must also run an efficient and cost-effective school."

The board embraced the challenge, and by the end of her first year, shared news not heard since the mid-1960s: A budget surplus was projected. Due to an increase in investment income and annual giving—and some good old-fashioned belt-tightening—Garrison Forest finished the 1990-91 year $122,000 in the black. Two decades later, the school has continued to balance its budget each year.

The time was right for another capital campaign, given Mrs. Bowman's reputation as a nationally recognized advocate for single-sex education and the need to raise $12 million for endowment and a fine and performing arts center. With a goal well beyond that of any previous GFS campaign, she and director of development Molly Hathaway began recruiting a national steering committee. This time, though, it was not the usual male leadership. It was an all-alumnae committee, many of whom had never been asked to support their alma mater in a leadership role or at a leadership level. "The campaign was a watershed moment for the school," Molly said. "We began traveling and personally engaging alumnae with their school. We had wonderful leadership from parents and men in the past, but this was about us coming of age." It was also a coming-of-age for the development program. Traveling for the first time to solicit gifts, Molly, Mrs. Bowman, and the campaign steering committee built relationships and awareness for Garrison Forest. Mrs. Bowman's musical avocation also enabled her to speak passionately of the need for a permanent home for Garrison Forest's fine and performing arts.

Trustees Betsy Searle '74 and Clare Springs '62 co-chaired the campaign. Noted Betsy, "It was clear that the primary resources were going to come from women, who were in more high-powered jobs and able to give back. The campaign resonated right away and was a frenzy once we started. The momentum was very exciting. We felt as if we were breaking through." During Mrs. Bowman's tenure, the campaign reached the halfway mark of its original $12 million goal. Ultimately, the campaign raised $22.3 million by 1998.

One of her first challenges ruffled more than a few feathers. Moore's Landing, the pond behind Meadowood, had long been home to flocks of

Middle School Latin teacher Joan McDonald (left) began the Roman Banquet tradition in 1977 as a capstone event for the eighth grade year. Held annually at Lochinvar for over a decade, the Roman Banquet was hosted by students for Middle School faculty and other invited adult guests. Hostesses and guests alike were clad in Roman garb for the celebration. After feasting on delicacies prepared by the students (or their parents), the evening concluded with fitting Roman entertainment, an exotic "belly dance."

For 25 years, Latin Day has celebrated the culmination of two years' study of Latin in the seventh and eighth grade. Held on alternate years at the Bryn Mawr or Garrison Forest School campuses, Latin Day commences with a luncheon banquet, continues with a drama contest and "Olympic" relay races, and concludes with the fiercely competitive chariot race. The Centennial year marks the silver anniversary running of this race.

Irene Jackson and her beloved geese.

geese, fed and cared for by Miss Irene Jackson. Some members of the community clung to the romantic notion that the fowl added to the picturesque quality of the Garrison Forest campus. Others felt the birds were simply foul. Though lovely to view from afar, the daily mess caused by the geese was a health hazard, and the geese were far from friendly. "Alex Uhle called them 'attack geese,' and one did run a small child around the pond before nipping him," Mrs. Bowman recalled. For the residential community, the noise could be more than annoying. One student recalled throwing her alarm clock at the geese from her dorm window in Meadowood to get them to stop their early morning honking in Penniman Park.

Convinced that the birds needed to leave, Mrs. Bowman contacted animal control at the Maryland State Department. "They humanely captured the geese, took them away, and found them a new home," Mrs. Bowman said. "It cost the school a lot of money, time, and red tape." Still, student rumors swirled that she had the geese killed and cooked for dinner at Lochinvar, a thought that gave her a laugh. Mr. Hodgetts also chuckled at how the expulsion of the campus geese was received. "It was a very sincere effort on Midge's part," he remarked. "But it was one of those cultural things and an amazing symbol of how life had been at the school."

"Residents" of Moore's Landing.

A few feathered friends were more than welcome at GFS, notably the young fowl in the 1992 Preschool production of "The Little Red Hen."

GOING GLOBAL

Another significant change was the shifting geographic make-up of the residential community. In fall 1990, among the 77 boarders enrolled, six were students from foreign countries. This was nothing new at Garrison Forest. Prior to World War II, U.S.-born boarders who lived outside the country had been enrolling in the school in small numbers. In the early 1990s, foreign-born students from Central America and Asia, along with U.S. citizens living in the Middle East, began attending GFS in growing numbers. "We received calls from non-English speaking families wanting to enroll, so we put together an 'English as a Second Language' program [the formal program began in 1993]," recalled Randie Benedict. "The international students were enormously brave and looked at the world in a different way. Students had stereotypes about people who live in other parts of the world that changed immediately in class and out of class. They figured out that teenagers around the world are very similar. They just speak different languages."

Yuko Taniguchi Wenzel '94 arrived on campus from Japan in 1991. "My first several months at GFS were challenging, to say the least," she reflected. "I didn't understand English, but more crucially, I didn't understand the culture. My memory of the first year is dealing with pressure, a feeling of being lost and lonely." The faculty and administration worked hard, Yuko said, to make sure that those international students who did not speak English as a native tongue were not left behind academically or socially. Three years later, Yuko was honored with the Faculty Award at graduation. There were some Garrison Forest traditions like New Girl initiation, though, which defied translation. "It is amusing in retrospect," Yuko recalled. "But it was actually a frightening experience at the time to be woken up in the middle of early morning and taken throughout the campus. My face was painted in blue and I had to place a pillow underneath my uniform all day. I looked quite strange, and I had no idea what was going on."

In the early 1990s, Garrison Forest became a leader in the Mid-Atlantic region for international boarding. Two decades later, students hailed from the Bahamas, China, France, Germany, Japan, Korea, Mexico, and other countries. A more global community on campus created an increased awareness of—and sensitivity to—the world beyond campus. "We were in the fledgling days of environmental education and globalization, and the international students were invaluable to that," noted Mrs. Bowman. "I felt that international students would have much to teach us."

Yuka Kanekubo Adamatsu '94 and Yuko Taniguchi Wenzel '94 leading the Art Club in a traditional Japanese tea ceremony.

Welcome sign for the new students in 2009.

Livingston students presenting their research on various countries during Morning Meeting.

With the country immersed in the first Gulf War, the school decided to cancel its planned spring break study trips to Russia and Spain for safety reasons. It also had everyday implications. "The advent of war in the Middle East has had a small but noticeable impact on school life," Mrs. Bowman reported to the board in January 1991. "Two of our boarders have family in Saudi Arabia, and it has been a tense time for them." Ms. Teaff organized a teach-in on the Middle East with experts, and Mrs. Smith, by then the school counselor, met with Lower School teachers on how to handle classroom questions. Rather than play constant TV coverage of a war that was broadcast around the clock, the school decided to cover discussions of the Gulf War in history classes. Students also conducted peace protests, and Amnesty International Club members wrote letters of support to U.S. soldiers.

During a 2009 GFS-sponsored trip to Spain, students visited El Alcázar in Segovia.

A WATERSHED MOMENT

On average, minority enrollment was 15 percent of the student body during the early 1990s. A growing number of students of color and international students with backgrounds and beliefs outside Garrison Forest's Christian traditions created a multicultural community. Like the rest of the country at the time, though, the school struggled with racial tension. On March 3, 1991, Rodney King, an African-American man, was beaten by four white Los Angeles police officers following a high-speed car chase. The event and the amateur video of the beating made headlines across the country.

That same spring, graffiti accusing a white student of racism was discovered in Marshall-Offutt. To address the heated emotions within the Upper School community, Mrs. Bowman cancelled morning classes for the day, and faculty and administrators led small group discussions on issues of race. A year later, another national event rippled across campus. On April 29, 1992, the four Los Angeles Police Department officers charged with assaulting Rodney King were acquitted during the state trial. Riots broke out in Los Angeles, and after six days, 53 people were dead and more than 7,000 were arrested. The campus discussions that followed prompted Mrs. Bowman to report to the trustees that "we must address the needs of our minority students to be heard and better understood."

Adopting the theme of diversity for the 1992-93 school year, she referenced the issue of race during her remarks at the opening faculty meeting. "I think it was clear to all of us that we must make an ongoing commitment to educate our students and ourselves about how to create a community where difference is respected and where all traditions have a place," she said. "We can no longer assume that GFS will be a place of tolerance and goodwill unless we make a conscious effort to teach and live these values."

On the morning of January 23, 1993, Dr. Burton Lee III, physician to the White House during George H. W. Bush's presidency, presented an assembly on AIDS to the Upper and Middle School students. What ensued created a defining moment about race at Garrison Forest. "Given his academic credentials and his public service background, it seemed like a real coup to bring him to GFS," Mrs. Bowman recalled. "It quickly became apparent that he had no feel for the age group he was addressing. Perhaps it was his dismissive response to some questions, [but] he lost the crowd." Dr. Lee's remarks focused on statistics about the origins of AIDS transmission from Africa. Several in attendance felt that his comments drifted from facts into innuendo,

Hanging out in the dorm with friends.

History teacher Beth Ruekberg, the school's first director of multicultural awareness, joined GFS in 1987.

Several classes in the 1990s wore AIDS ribbons at Commencement.

The 1993 King and Queen of Snoball, a winter dance for juniors and seniors.

disparaging different national, ethnic, and racial groups, particularly urban African-American women. During the assembly, several girls and teachers walked out of Garland Theater in protest. [The Garrison Forest Archives does not have a copy of his speech.]

"I was in total shock," recalled Ebony Terrell Cooper '93, who was senior class boarding president and one of the founders of the Black Student Union, which was created shortly after the assembly. "Many students of all races and backgrounds were upset as were faculty members. It was not a black and white issue." Dr. Lee's remarks and the reaction to them dominated discussion in and out of class for the rest of the day. The next day, Ebony and classmates Nikkia Rowe and Xiomara Edwards wore all black in protest.

"The assembly with Dr. Lee was a horrible morning from which came a huge step forward in addressing the issues of diversity," reflected Beth Ruekberg, history teacher. "The community became healthier and safer as a result. Crises are good, if they are managed well, to move the school forward. We needed to address the needs of all students and teach all students the greatness of our diversity."

Mrs. Bowman concurred: "Dr. Lee catalyzed something that was there already." In the weeks following the assembly, she hired national diversity consultants to work with the school on diversity issues and conflict resolution, and appointed Ms. Ruekberg as director of the newly created office of multicultural awareness. The consultants also recommended the creation and adoption of a Statement of Respect. "Midge sought collaboration," Ms. Ruekberg said. "She brought faculty, administrators, and consultants together to come up with an action plan and move us forward."

The school created diversity programs, including a fall 1993 QUEST overnight camping trip for the Upper School focused on diversity, and the creation of the Bridge Program to help new students of all races and backgrounds orient themselves to Garrison Forest. In the following years, students established the Jewish Student Alliance, the International Student Alliance, and the Gay/Straight Student Alliance. The Gay/Straight Faculty and Staff Alliance was created in 2008. The year prior, the school inaugurated Community Connections Day, during which the Lower Division, Middle School, and Upper School gather to discuss diversity. "Dr. Lee's visit under-scored for me how much the school had changed and that we were ready for true diversity," Randie Benedict remarked. "We had an assumed expectation but never articulated what that was. The Statement of Respect put us in a position to be welcoming and good stewards to everyone in the community."

At the start of its centennial academic year, both the percentage of students of color and administrators of color are well above the national averages. "Diversity work is always in progress," remarked Malika DeLancey, director of multicultural affairs. "There is no beginning and no end. There are many groups for students and adults in our community that are based on cultural affinity. We have a significant number of students of color, and we have a thriving residential program that includes young women from all around the world. We are continuing to make strides, but there will always be work to do. Specific goals include increasing our faculty of color numbers and including diversity throughout the curriculum."

The Statement of Respect was adopted in 1993, which created the foundation for the school to expand its definition of diversity beyond race.

The Garrison Forest School community is deeply committed to equity, honesty, kindness, and respect as part of the educational experience. To this end, we:

• celebrate diversity both within our community and our curriculum;

• are concerned for the well-being of all people;

• seek to build the self-esteem of all people;

• aspire to promote the understanding of all people.

We recognize the dignity and worth of all individuals. To protect their rights, we confront bias, prejudice, and discrimination. Garrison Forest School does not condone any behavior which is inconsistent with these tenets. We believe that it is unacceptable for our spoken and written language and behavior to demean anyone's physical characteristics, as well as anyone's ethnic, gender, personal, racial, religious, or sexual identities. We, as individuals, must take responsibility for our words and deeds and respect all people.

The first Community Connections Day in 2007.

PREPARING FOR THE 21ST CENTURY

As the school grappled with issues of race and developed policies and programs to create a more accepting environment, Mrs. Bowman and the board continued to focus on the educational accomplishments and challenges of the day. The Middle School had grown from 76 to 100 students in four years, and the school had been carefully and strategically strengthening its curricula in science and math. One-hundred percent of seniors were graduating with four years of math, the Middle School science program was revised, and the Lower School math sequence was upgraded, based on the Johns Hopkins Gifted and Talented program. These early connections with Johns Hopkins were precursors to the school's partnership with Hopkins in 2005 to create the Women in Science and Engineering (WISE) program, which offers hands-on mentorships in JHU labs to GFS juniors and seniors.

As a small group of faculty was going online via a modem through Baltimore's public library system to the still relatively unknown Internet, the school's first Technology Committee was formed in 1993 to study future technological needs and uses. Shortly thereafter, the library card catalog was digitized.

In June 1994, Mrs. Bowman returned to her hometown of Seattle after four years as headmistress. She left the school with thriving enrollments in all four divisions, including successful international and eighth grade boarding programs, and a better sense and acceptance of the people who comprised the growing Garrison Forest community. In announcing Mrs. Bowman's resignation to the broader community, board president Grant Hathaway wrote that "during her tenure, the school experienced a period of solid growth in all areas…[and] as an educational leader, [she] has strengthened public awareness of Garrison Forest as a school whose academic excellence is recognized both nationally and internationally."

Her words to the faculty at the closing faculty meeting reflected her intellect and her feelings about her time at Garrison Forest. She chose two Greek words that describe different concepts of time: *Chronos* for chronological time; and *Khairos*, which she called "sacred time: of the spirit, the heart, unmeasurable but real." By *Chronos* measurements, she noted, her time at Garrison Forest had been short. "But my years here have been rich in *Khairos*."

Joan Mudge began her GFS career as a history teacher in 1969. In 1984, Mrs. Underwood tapped her to become the school's first full-time college counselor, a position she held until her retirement in 2007. Mrs. Mudge also served as dean of faculty. Upon retirement, she embarked on a painting career, which has included several shows at GFS, while continuing as a consultant to the school's college counseling office.

SPIRITED SERVICE

Service League and Miss Marshall and Miss Offutt, harvesting corn during World War II on the family farm of Kitty Anne Ballard Cover '48.

Among the earliest community service efforts at Garrison Forest were the GFS "Farmerettes" (top right) working in fields during World War I and student collections to support various causes during the 1920s. Reaching beyond oneself to the larger world was intrinsic to the high moral ideals and strength of character that Miss Livingston desired in her students. During the next war, a group of juniors and seniors wanted to find a way for the school to help on the home front and abroad. In 1942, with Miss Marshall and Miss Offutt's blessing, students drew up a charter, and within days, the school's first Service League was founded. Early activities included selling war stamps and bonds, filling Christmas stockings for soldiers, and again, harvesting corn on nearby farms while farmers were off fighting in World War II.

The longest continually running student organization, Service League has expanded greatly since its earliest days to support local, national, and international causes. Never a requirement by the school, community service is embraced by the student body and embodied in the meaning of *Esse Quam Videri*—To Be Rather Than To Seem. Service League's impact has created greater altruistic ripples within the school community that inspire individual and non-Service League outreach, as well as a host of perennial Service League projects. "When we created Service League, community service was very definitely a part of our lives," recalled Kitty Chaplin Martin '43, one of the original Service League board members. "You were expected to help others. Miss Marshall and Miss Offutt wanted us to be whole people."

The "Farmerettes"

Immediately following the 2004 Hurricane Katrina and Asian tsunami tragedies, the Upper School led collections for the Red Cross during carpool "bucket brigades."

DONALD BENTLEY FOOD PANTRY

For over a decade, Middle School students have spearheaded the school's support of the Donald Bentley Food Pantry in East Baltimore. Established in 1990 by area high school students, the food pantry commemorates the life of Donald Bentley, a Gilman graduate who was killed in a robbery attempt in 1989. Middle School students collect non-perishable food items and deliver them to the pantry throughout the year as well as sponsor a school-wide "Stuff the Bus" can drive in the fall and a spring contest among Middle School advisory groups.

SUSAN G. KOMEN RACE FOR THE CURE

In 1995, the GFS-sponsored Girl Scout troop walked around campus to support the Susan G. Komen Race for the Cure, raising $2,000 for breast cancer research (above). Two years later, "Team GFS" was participating in the actual Maryland Komen race. In 2009, the 500 GFS team members raised nearly $20,000, and David Berdan, Lower Division and Middle School science teacher, won the Maryland Komen 5K race in 16:17 minutes.

Volunteering at Baltimore County General Hospital, 1967.

GFS students and families have supported Rebuilding Together: Baltimore, beginning in the 2000s.

HEAD START

In 1965, Mrs. Montgomery applied for and received a federal grant to create a Head Start program through St. Thomas' Church, held during the summers in Manor House. Day students volunteered in the program, which was outside the purview of Service League, and served upward of 40 children.

I Volunteered for Habitat for Humanity

HABITAT FOR HUMANITY

The school's response to Hurricane Katrina in 2004 included the sponsorship of a Habitat for Humanity house, which benefited a New Orleans family who had relocated to Baltimore. Led by the adults in the GFS community, the school annually sponsors a Habitat house. Pictured are members of the GFS work team (left to right): Peggy O'Neill, Butch Darrell, Beth Ruekberg, Kim Marlor, Kathy Schaffer, and Mr. O'Neill.

OUR DAILY BREAD

Garrison Forest has supported Our Daily Bread, a meal program in Baltimore, since the 1980s. Older students coordinate serving meals through the school's membership in the Baltimore-wide Students Sharing Coalition. In 2008, Livingston students began a tradition of making and bagging lunches for Our Daily Bread as part of the GFS Halloween festivities.

THE ELSIE FOSTER JENKINS '53
COMMUNITY SERVICE ENDOWMENT FUND

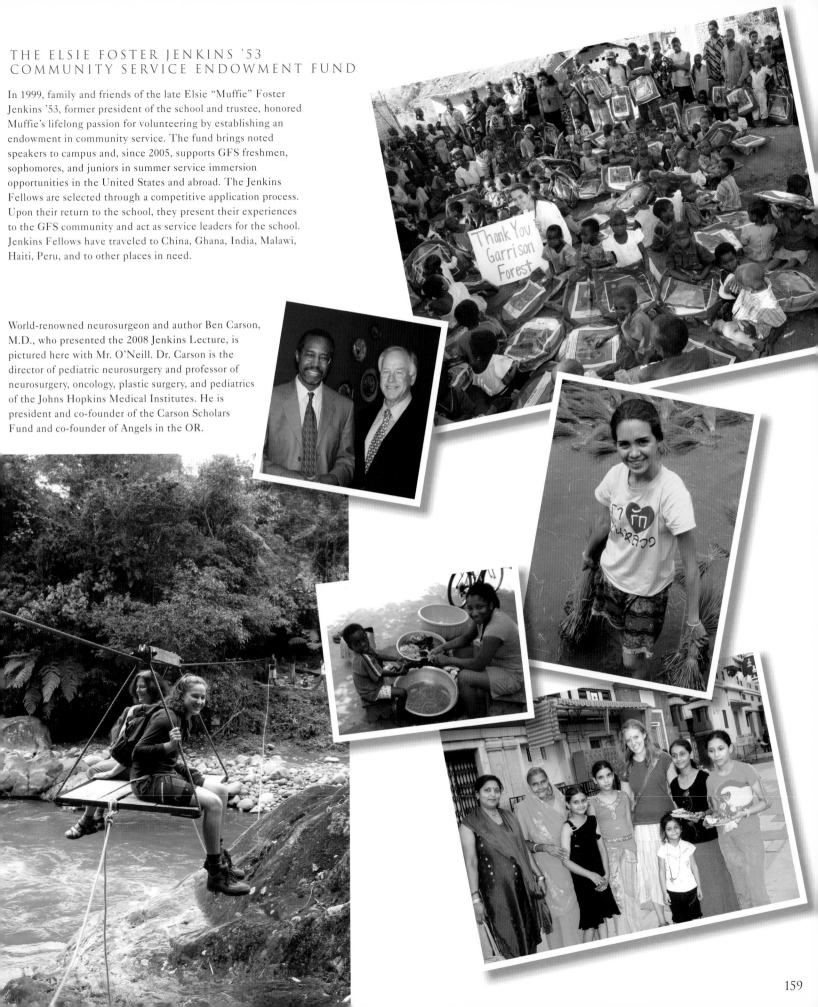

In 1999, family and friends of the late Elsie "Muffie" Foster Jenkins '53, former president of the school and trustee, honored Muffie's lifelong passion for volunteering by establishing an endowment in community service. The fund brings noted speakers to campus and, since 2005, supports GFS freshmen, sophomores, and juniors in summer service immersion opportunities in the United States and abroad. The Jenkins Fellows are selected through a competitive application process. Upon their return to the school, they present their experiences to the GFS community and act as service leaders for the school. Jenkins Fellows have traveled to China, Ghana, India, Malawi, Haiti, Peru, and to other places in need.

World-renowned neurosurgeon and author Ben Carson, M.D., who presented the 2008 Jenkins Lecture, is pictured here with Mr. O'Neill. Dr. Carson is the director of pediatric neurosurgery and professor of neurosurgery, oncology, plastic surgery, and pediatrics of the Johns Hopkins Medical Institutes. He is president and co-founder of the Carson Scholars Fund and co-founder of Angels in the OR.

Middle schoolers, 2008.

G. PETER O'NEILL, JR.
HEAD OF SCHOOL, 1994-

G. Peter O'Neill, Jr. had very definite expectations when he agreed to interview for the position of interim head of Garrison Forest School in 1994. If offered the job, he would stay the required one year, and then return to New England, his beloved Boston Red Sox, and the coeducational independent school world where he had spent 23 years as an administrator, teacher, and coach. He thought that a yearlong stint at GFS would be an interesting, albeit brief, professional challenge in single-sex education, nothing more.

All that changed when he set foot on campus for the first time. "I sensed the difference right away," said Mr. O'Neill, who received his bachelor's from St. Michael's College and master's from Trinity College. "That first day, I met girls who had an unaffected sense of self-confidence. I had not seen that in my previous career in coed settings." At Morning Meeting, he watched announcements and a few silly skits, standard fare for the start of a school day at Garrison Forest. "The skits would not have been possible in a coed setting," he commented. "They were entirely appropriate, and now I realize were critical to a healthy environment for girls to be able to have that freedom to express themselves."

But it was the answer he received to a question he posed to his student tour guide that changed his expectations about Garrison Forest. "I asked her, 'What is the best thing about Garrison Forest?' and she said, 'The people and the teachers.' That was it. It was the community, everyone's first response when asked about what he or she valued about the school. That is certainly what I've come to value as well."

A few months later, on July 1, 1994, the Philadelphia-born, New Jersey-raised educator began his intended year-long position as interim head. As the school celebrates its Centennial in 2010, Mr. O'Neill celebrates his 16th year at Garrison Forest, the third longest head of school tenure in GFS history. His cheerful countenance, approachable demeanor, charisma, and enthusiasm are balanced by an attentiveness to the individual and institution—qualities that have been instrumental in the

Mr. O'Neill, 1994.

Light Blue and Dark Blue notwithstanding, Mr. O'Neill is partial to the Boston Red Sox's team colors.

In December 2009, China's Hanban Institute selected GFS as a Confucius Classroom, Maryland's first independent school to receive the honor. Hanban funding includes a Chinese teacher of Mandarin Chinese and cultural enrichment resources. Since 2006, students from China have been part of the school's thriving global community.

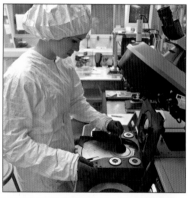

Garrison Forest WISE students at The Johns Hopkins University, fabricating nanodisks (above) and using the DaVinci Robot (bottom).

school's accomplishments under his tutelage. He has overseen the largest campus expansion phase to date with approximately $30 million of improvements from 1994-2008, including an extensive technology program. With a talent for fundraising and the business of running a school, Mr. O'Neill has worked closely with the board and school leaders to create a fiscally sound institution. From 1994 to 2009, the endowment increased from $6 million to $32 million, the Annual Fund surpassed the $1.25 million mark, and the budget remained balanced. Enrollment grew to nearly 700 students in 2009—a long way from the two dozen or so original students in 1910.

Innovation has been a hallmark of the recent decades at Garrison Forest. In 2005, the school introduced the Women in Science and Engineering (WISE) program in partnership with The Johns Hopkins University to offer hands-on lab mentorships with Hopkins professors and graduate students. Two years later, GFS received an inaugural Edward E. Ford Foundation Leadership Challenge Grant to create the James Center: Programs and Partnerships with a Public Purpose. The James Center offers leadership programs, coordinates Service League and other service learning projects, provides education and experiential opportunities on financial literacy, and oversees the WISE program.

Mr. O'Neill and the trustees redefined the school's residential program to create more flexible components that meet the demands of a 21st century day/residential school. While GFS continues to have traditional resident students from across the United States and increasingly around the globe, the school created short-term and regional boarding options in the late 1990s, which include leadership training programs, semester-based programs, and the WISE program. A century after Miss Livingston welcomed the first boarders into extra rooms in the school's only building, virtually all Upper School students experience a residential component to their Garrison Forest education, a real benefit before going to college.

Following in the footsteps of his modern GFS predecessors, Mr. O'Neill became a national leader as an advocate for girls' education. In 1995, he was elected to the decidedly feminine-titled Headmistresses Association of the East. A decade later, he served as president of the Association of Independent Maryland Schools (AIMS), has been a trustee and treasurer of the National Coalition of Girls' Schools (NCGS), and served on the board of the National Association of Principals of Schools for Girls. In 2006, the Klingenstein Center at Columbia University recognized him as one of the country's outstanding school heads. "Peter is one of the standard-bearers nationally for male heads of girls' schools," remarked GFS's Whitney Ransome, director of the James Center. "His national profile not only showcases him as a leader but showcases GFS as an incubator for innovation."

FINDING COMMUNITY

As Mr. O'Neill began his interim year, the board mounted a national search for his permanent replacement. A few months into the search, search committee chair Anne Van Ingen '73, her fellow trustees, and others felt they already had their candidate—and he was already doing the job. Said Mr. Hodgetts, "There was no question that Peter was the best candidate. Fairly quickly, it became clear that it was a great fit." But Mr. O'Neill declined the board's mid-year invitation to throw his hat in the ring, choosing to honor his original commitment to stay for one year. Though he had found Garrison Forest a good match professionally and personally, he was concerned about his gender. "I was not entirely sure that a man should head a girls' school," he admits. "Men as heads of girls' schools should be the rare exception and never the rule. It's essential that the vast majority of role models within the school be women. However, early on at Garrison Forest, I became aware that if girls only saw women, they might begin to think that men did not take the education of young women seriously. I try to speak to their intelligence, competitiveness, assertion, and ability to test themselves, not how popular culture values them." Happily in the gender-minority at the school, he jokes that male faculty—11 percent of the total GFS faculty in 2009-10—are enough for a basketball team with few substitutions.

Elizabeth "Zibby" Andrews, head of the Lower Division, greets a student in a GFS tradition that can be traced back to the days of Miss Livingston.

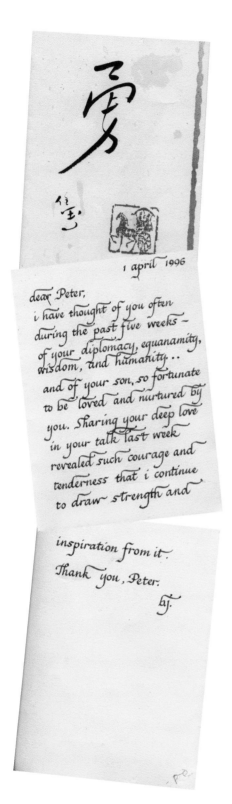

愛

1 april 1996

dear Peter,
i have thought of you often
during the past five weeks –
of your diplomacy, equanamity,
wisdom, and humanity..
and of your son, so fortunate
to be loved and nurtured by
you. Sharing your deep love
in your talk last week
revealed such courage and
tenderness that i continue
to draw strength and

inspiration from it.
Thank you, Peter.

bj.

Following Mr. O'Neill's remarks to the school community, art department chair B.J. McElderry penned this note.

Male heads of girls' schools were atypical in the mid-1990s, a significant departure from the landscape of girls' school leadership just a decade prior when the majority of heads were male. For the on-campus community, the issue was not gender but fit. "Peter was more self-conscious about it than we were," noted Ms. Teaff. "What faculty and administrators wanted was a good head. He wasn't afraid to put the issue of his gender on the table." The trustees knew that he was the right person for the job. "He came into GFS, and we just watched him fall in love with the school," recalled Elinor Purves McLennan '56.

Grant Hathaway, president of the board when Mr. O'Neill was hired as interim head, and the search committee were convinced that gender or any other difference should not be an influence when choosing the most qualified candidate. "Peter's demonstration of leadership, honest approach, and engaging personality clearly made him the right choice," Mr. Hathaway noted. As Mr. O'Neill's interim year drew to a close, the search had yet to produce a successful candidate. The board asked Mr. O'Neill to serve for another year as interim head. By early February 1995, the search was postponed, and the trustees approached him again and asked if he would agree to a third year. "I said that I would stay on for the foreseeable future, but I still was not envisioning a long-term tenure."

While mulling over his future and what role Garrison Forest might have in it, tragedy struck. On February 25, 1996, Colin, his only child from Mr. O'Neill's first marriage, died during a surfing accident while attending Middlebury College's study abroad program in Costa Rica. Shortly after Mr. O'Neill returned to campus from the funeral, he spoke candidly to the Upper School about his son. His choice to speak—and his moving choice of words— was a conscious "teachable moment" for the former classroom teacher. "I knew the students were going to struggle with how to deal with me [after Colin died], and I wanted to reassure them that that wasn't their job," he said. That morning, in addition to the stories he shared of Colin, he offered suggestions of how students might interact with him and not feel uncomfortable. "I told them that it was okay to laugh around me, that it was okay to be natural, to be themselves, in fact, that would help me more than anything," he recalled. "I also wanted to give the message that it is so critically important for them to connect to those in their lives, and to give them the message that they were sacredly valued by their parents and others. I asked that they take a moment that day, and many of them did, just to tell someone, particularly a parent, what he or she meant to them."

Edie Horney, then dean of students, praised the way he handled his grief with the students. "It was very painful for him, but the students learned so

much." She described the school's support of him as being part of the
Garrison Forest spirit. "It is not just what we can do for you, but that we are
here for one another. The school has always been a family." Rev. William
Baxter, former St. Thomas' rector and GFS school chaplain from 1994-1997
and again from 1999-2007, added, "Peter's walk through grief and beyond
was a powerful lesson to all in the GFS community."

Experiencing such a devastating loss while being part of the school
cemented his decision to remain at GFS. "I knew this was a place I needed
to be for as long as the community would have me and as long as I felt I
could continue to make a contribution," Mr. O'Neill said. "The school
embraced me in ways that I think, would not, and could not have possibly
occurred in another setting. When I lost Colin, this community helped to
save my life."

This photograph of Colin O'Neill sailing,
an interest he shared with his father,
graces the Livingston lobby with the
words, "This building is dedicated to
the memory of Colin T. O'Neill, whose
life has touched this school through his
father." This dedication is at the request
of the GFS family that supported the
renovation and construction of the former
Study Hall into Livingston, which was
built shortly after Colin's death. In the
photo, Colin is at the helm of a tall ship as
part of a semester-at-sea program prior to
attending Middlebury.

Lochinvar has served as the setting for the prom for several classes. Pictured here is the Class of 2004.

Mr. and Mrs. O'Neill, always cheering for GFS.

EMBRACING FAMILY

In 1998, Mr. O'Neill became part of a long GFS tradition of having a family living in the head's residence when he married Peggy Foley, who had two sons, Paul and Sean, and a young daughter, Cara. Mrs. O'Neill, a former independent school business manager, immediately became a positive force for change on campus and a ready partner for her husband's vision for the school. She established an on-campus daycare for faculty and staff, created the school's first-ever organized archives, and oversaw the creation of a new student center in the former dining facilities in Manor House. Called the O'Zone in her honor, the center is a popular gathering place for Middle and Upper School students throughout the week. The O'Neills continued the tradition of opening up Lochinvar for everything from the prom to trustee dinners and capital campaign celebrations. They expanded the annual holiday party for faculty and staff to include every member of the staff and continued the Lochinvar tradition of music and dancing at many events.

An old hand at first days at Garrison Forest, Mr. O'Neill walked Cara to her first day of third grade in fall 1998. A decade later, he handed Cara, a member of the Class of 2008, her Garrison Forest diploma. It is his proudest GFS moment, he happily admits. "Truly the high point of my tenure, and most meaningful for me, was watching Cara grow up here and benefit enormously from her experience at Garrison Forest," he said. "I gained an even deeper appreciation for the quality of a GFS experience in seeing it through her life and eyes." Having a parent as head of one's school is a unique challenge, one he says she handled with aplomb: "It helped that she had a different last name, but there were often years when new students would arrive, and some of them wouldn't realize that I was her stepfather until halfway through the year. She would call 'Peter' across the dining room, and they would be horrified."

An area where he was particularly conscious of his dual role as GFS parent and head of school was on the athletic sidelines. Cara was a three-sport athlete in field hockey, basketball, and lacrosse. "I think one of the more challenging aspects of my position was trying to maintain the standards that I expect of our other parents in the mix of heated athletic contests," he admitted. "Being a competitive person, having played a fair number of sports and coached them, and having just enough knowledge to be dangerous, is not an easy thing. I'd occasionally get chided by fellow parents—or, most often, Peggy—when I got a little too passionate about an official's call or how the game was going. They would remind me that as parents, we're supposed to be 'appropriate' on the sidelines."

BUILDING A FUTURE

During Mr. O'Neill's first visit to Garrison Forest, after passing horse pastures, the elegant Robinswood, and green trees, he was surprised to see a large, white pipe connecting the former stables and maintenance shed to the Little Gym. The pipe was about 12 feet off the ground, had peeling white paint, and was partially wrapped in duct tape. It was also directly across from the visitors' parking lot. "My first thought was, 'What is that?' though I didn't quite say it that way," he joked. "I did not have any idea then that the goal of my whole tenure would be to remove the white pipe."

Later he came to learn that the pipe was the source of heat for the maintenance building and had been a highly visible architectural element of the campus since the Little Gym was built in 1920. The building was

With stepdaughter Cara Foley on her first day at GFS in 1998.

Mr. and Mrs. O'Neill and Cara at her graduation in 2008.

A fly-fisherman and fan of the Norman Maclean novella, *A River Runs Through It*, and subsequent film of the same name, Mr. O'Neill directed his own version entitled "A Bulldozer Runs Through It" in 1995. That year, the maintenance shed (the original GFS stables) was razed to make room for the new Fine and Performing Arts Center.

There she goes!

used by Stan Zolenas's preschool physical education classes. "If Stan had let his kindergartners, they could have leaned against it and knocked it down," Mr. O'Neill laughs. "When I arrived, Garrison Forest had a backlog of facility needs that began with the white pipe," he explains. A campaign was under way to raise money for a fine and performing arts center, and he became a vocal supporter of the need to integrate into one building the school's outstanding, but physically scattered, programs. "Peter was very much an agent for change, yet he was able to bridge and acknowledge and respect the traditions that had gone on," noted Bill Hodgetts, assistant head of school for finance and operations.

Dubbing 1995 "The Year of the Hard Hat," Mr. O'Neill and the board began the process of building the arts center, which required leveling the maintenance shed, a process that took about 15 minutes, chuckled Mr. O'Neill. He witnessed the building being razed and savored each bulldozer pass. Later, to make room for the Campus Center, the Little Gym met the same fate, albeit with a little more style. "When we took down the Little Gym, we had a decommissioning ceremony complete with Bill Baxter as our chaplain, to send the building to its greater reward," Mr. O'Neill said.

As construction continued, the board developed an overall master plan, which was revised several times. Since 1995, the school has built or renovated the Lower School, now called Livingston; and added a collegiate-quality riding center, the D. & J. Smith Equestrian Center; a state-of-the-art athletic center, the Elizabeth B. Searle '74 Athletic Center with the adjacent Alumnae Hall dining facility; two turf fields; and the Silver LEED-certified Middle School. Every older building on campus received a needed face-lift. "At each stage of the process, we also were improving faculty salaries, benefits, professional development, and faculty housing," Mr. O'Neill explained. "The facilities were improved not to create programs, but to match the quality of the program that already existed."

Near-constant construction brought challenges, but he relished it, joking that, at first, about the only other people who enjoyed the construction to the degree he did were the preschool boys. Again, embracing the "teachable moments," he and the faculty began talking with the girls about the construction process from architectural and engineering stand-points, particularly about the green building practices used for the Middle School.

STEERING THROUGH CHALLENGES

As the events of September 11, 2001, tragically unfolded, Mr. O'Neill and his administrators and trustees made a careful, though at the time controversial, decision. As many of their peer institutions across the region were cancelling classes, Garrison Forest remained open for the day, only cancelling afternoon activities. "We determined within probably the first hour that we had a parent of a resident student involved in the World Trade Centers, and that made a critical difference," he explained. "There were all kinds of rumors circulating, and we felt students were safest first and foremost here, although we did allow parents, of course, to pick up their children, and a number did."

He quickly called a faculty meeting and informed the adults that the school would monitor reports, but the event would not be shown on TV at school where students could see it. That decision was based on the fact that, at the time, the student's mother was unaccounted for in the World Trade Center; a few days later she was confirmed dead.

Teachers were encouraged to talk openly but carefully about the information. That evening, Mr. O'Neill gathered the residential community and talked with them in the dining hall, and faculty and staff met with students in the residence halls that night. "We did not hide from it, we acknowledged that it was an extraordinary tragedy," he said. "We knew that this was going to be one of the most profound experiences in the lives of the children we had in our charge, but we could not traumatize them." At Morning Meeting the next day, the Upper School gathered in prayer for the nation and those who lost family members during the attacks.

"Peter made an excellent decision," Beth Ruekberg, chair of the history department, said. "He was prudent in not setting up TVs. I had a student who was very angry about that, but we needed to have normalcy knowing that we had kids whose parents were in the World Trade Center and Pentagon." Erica Chan '02 reflected on the day's events, noting that "the school stood strong and supportive for those directly affected, and I remember thinking how lucky I was to be part of such a great community."

An alumna, Karen Hagerty '85, also lost her life when the World Trade Center collapsed. She was in the second tower waiting for the elevator, joking with her co-workers that after the people with children evacuated, she should go next because she had a cat waiting for her at home. Her body shielded the man who survived to tell the tale, said her cousin Jane Suren Harrington '60.

Karen Hagerty '85, who perished in the September 11 attacks on the World Trade Center, pictured here in her yearbook photo.

The O'Zone café in Manor House was named for Mrs. O'Neill.

In honor of the new "green" Middle School, seedling packets were distributed during the 2006 Parents' Weekend "Greenbreaking."

The next fall, the school took an equally balanced approach to keep students safe during the Washington D.C. sniper attacks. School leaders assessed site lines from Reisterstown Road and created an escort system for students moving between buildings, but chose not to keep students inside or cancel outdoor events, as a number of schools did. Following these events, the school re-revaluated its security and added surveillance cameras and more security guards.

Four years later, Hurricane Katrina's devastation of New Orleans also engendered compassion from the GFS community. The students in all divisions organized a bucket brigade fundraiser in every carpool. Shortly after the tragedy, Middle School teacher Butch Darrell came into Mr. O'Neill's office to talk about how the school might respond. "I told Peter that we need to do something to help the people in Louisiana, but that there was a huge need to help the homeless in Baltimore as well," recalls Mr. Darrell. "We need to commit ourselves to correcting that situation here, right here in our community." His vision led to the school partnering with the Sandtown Habitat for Humanity (Baltimore's chapter). By 2009, Garrison Forest faculty, staff, trustees, and alumnae, had rehabbed four houses in Baltimore's underserved Sandtown-Winchester neighborhood. Fittingly, the first house was given to a family who relocated from New Orleans following Hurricane Katrina. GFS volunteers work on weekends year-round, with GFS Service League running a day camp on campus for the workers' children. Through the GFS Habitat program, the adults model volunteerism for the students.

The 2009 *Ragged Robin* yearbook, which was dedicated to Mr. O'Neill (pictured left with the Class of 2009), took its theme from his yearly fish-stories-as-educational-metaphors. Part of the dedication states: "Mr. O'Neill leads by example; his greatest accomplishments have been fulfilled with integrity and modeled after our School motto, *Esse Quam Videri*—To Be and Not to Seem. Perhaps this is the greatest lesson he has taught us."

A STORYTELLER

Mr. O'Neill's stories are an anticipated (and expected) part of his rousing beginning-of-the-year speeches to the faculty and inspiring words to graduates at Commencement. He peppers Morning Meeting or dinner-time announcements with amusing tales about fishing or other topics, with crackerjack timing and good-natured self-deprecation. Anecdotes often poke fun at his stereotypical "guy" moments as the male head of an all-girls' school, such as his love for campus construction and his fly-and deep-sea fishing adventures. A favorite story involved some hands-on help for the field hockey team. At 9 a.m. on a Saturday morning, he and the varsity squad stood on the sidelines of the GFS playing fields. A very wet fall and a too-early-in-the-week mowing had left the fields looking like something akin to shag carpeting. In one hour, the field hockey team was scheduled to host

Ann Gray, "the boss of the Preschool," and Mr. O'Neill, "the boss of the whole school," welcome new GFS students to the school.

Mr. O'Neill behind the wheel.

an interscholastic tournament. The grass was unplayable. One of the varsity co-captains turned to him and asked if there were any way he could get the grass mowed. Mr. O'Neill hurried to the maintenance building, and via phone, got a quick lesson from an off-duty grounds crew member on handling the school's very large riding mower. By the time the tournament was scheduled to start, Mr. O'Neill had mowed the grass to the perfect length for regulation play, enjoying every minute of the ride: "The lawn mower was a biggie and a ball to drive."

But his favorite story involves one of his earliest, and perhaps biggest, lessons in leading a girls' school. When he was introduced to a class of four-year-old boys and girls, teacher Valerie Marsh asked if the children knew what Mr. O'Neill's job was. "A whole group of hands went up, and the boys were half out of their seats, jumping up and waving," he recalls. A boy answered first, announcing that then head of the Preschool, Mrs. [Ann] Gray was the "boss of the Preschool, but Mr. O'Neill was the boss of the whole school."

Mr. O'Neill smiled at the comment, but reflected on the larger issue implicit in the boy's comments: "In one gender-specific moment, he had de-fined leadership as hierarchical, authoritarian, and that authority comes from title. And he also understood a flow chart." Ms. Marsh replied that, yes that is some of it, but asked the children if there was more to Mr. O'Neill's job. "I will never forget that a girl raised her hand, and as she was called on, she very simply said, 'He takes care of the school.'" To me that has been the definition of my job," he noted. "To her, leadership was relationship-based and about supporting things, not authoritarian or hierarchical. Yes, there has to be a degree of authority, but it has to be well shared and very collaborative. I did come to find that my most important job was taking care of the school."

For Mr. O'Neill, he has defined his job—and the success of the school— through happy and effective partnerships with his first three board chairs: Betsy Searle '74, Molly Mundy Hathaway '61, and Lila Boyce Lohr '63. "What has been accomplished has been in collaboration with the board and the three exceptional women who have led it," Mr. O'Neill noted.

It is a partnership that is preparing Garrison Forest School for its next century of spirit. Reflecting on Mr. O'Neill's tenure and service to the school, Lila, who began her presidency in 2005, noted that, "Peter's passion for excellence in education, his experience and vision, his ability to connect with every part of this community, and his dedication to the mission of Garrison Forest have positioned us perfectly to begin our next century with strength, purpose, and pride."

In this historic picture with President of the Board of Trustees Lila Boyce Lohr '63 (far left), are former presidents who represent nearly 40 years of trustee leadership. Relie Garland Bolton '53 (far right) became the first woman president in 1968. Others who led and served with distinction were (left to right) Molly Mundy Hathaway '61, Fred Whitridge, Betsy Searle '74, Grant Hathaway, and Elinor Purves McLennan '56. Not pictured: Peyton "Skippy" Cochran, Jr.

GROWING A CAMPUS

The Garrison Forest campus during its Centennial year would be barely recognizable to the school's founding headmistress and families. Over the decades, buildings have been added—and razed—to accommodate growth in the student and faculty bodies, the academic, arts, and athletic programs, and to meet the educational challenges of the day, such as technology. In 2010, the Garrison Forest campus encompasses 110 acres and an array of academic, residential, and athletic facilities. The largest capital expansion in the history of the school occurred under Mr. O'Neill's tutelage. From 1994-2007, the school added several new buildings, renovated older facilities, fully wired the campus for technology, and completed the master plan that created a pedestrian campus.

At the Campus Center opening, 2002 and the Campus Center (below).

The former New or Big Gym,
now the Old Gym.

CAMPUS CENTER

In 2002, the school added the Campus Center, which houses the
Elizabeth B. Searle '74 Athletic Center (SAC) and Alumnae Hall
dining facility. At the time of its opening, the SAC was one of the
premier health and fitness facilities of its kind among girls' schools
nationwide. Named for trustee and standout GFS athlete Betsy
Searle, the SAC and its adjacent turf fields also recognize two men and
"living legends" in the annals of Grizzly sports: history teacher and
consummate coach Butch Darrell, for whom the basketball courts
are named; and longtime Lower Division physical education teacher
Stan Zolenas or "Mr. Z.," for whom the Zolenas Turf Field was
dedicated in 2008.

Ingredients:
12 pieces of chicken, cut-up
1 t. Season-All
½ t. garlic powder
½ t. cayenne pepper
½ t. salt
½ t. pepper
½ t. Old Bay Seasoning
½ t. onion salt
2 cups flour
1½ t. paprika

IRVIN'S FRIED CHICKEN

The day before serving the chicken, mix seasoning together except the paprika and flour. Liber-
ally coat the chicken pieces with the seasoning mix. Place in a bag or sealed container and
refrigerate overnight.

On day two, mix the paprika and flour together and coat the seasoned chicken pieces. Shake off
the excess flour and fry each piece in peanut or vegetable oil, turning about halfway through.
Drain well on a rack.

NOTE: Mr. McGregor estimates 12-15 minutes for breast and wing pieces and 18-20 minutes for
other pieces. Serves 12, though Mr. McGregor's recipe at GFS called for 250 pieces of chicken.

Mr. O'Neill is assisted in the Alumnae Hall ribbon-cutting by dining
hall staff Irvin McGregor, Connie Mann, and Theresa Skinner.
Mr. McGregor's delicious food, kindness, and laid-back manner were
beloved by the GFS community during the 43 years he worked at the
school. His chicken recipe is a favorite of alumnae, students, faculty,
and staff, and is served at many school festivities. The new kitchen
in the Alumnae Hall was named "Irvin's Place" in his honor, and the
school established an award for staff service in his honor. Mrs. Skinner
has been a constant, welcoming presence at GFS since 1971.

MIDDLE SCHOOL

In 2007, Garrison Forest inaugurated its first green, Silver Leadership in Energy and Environmental Design (LEED) certified building, the new Middle School. Blending sustainable construction practices and academic technology with architecture echoing the gracious lines of Manor House, the Middle School was designed with the needs of 21st-century adolescent learners. The building offers plenty of space for collaborative learning and self-expression, while anchoring the students in the classical roots of a Garrison Forest education. Latin phrases are emblazoned as permanent features above the entrance to each hallway portal, including *Non mihi, non tibi, sed nobis,* (Not for me, not for you, but for us), which remind the students to look beyond themselves.

New Middle School
"Greenbreaking"
October 20, 2006

Cedar Tree

Middle School Head Steve McManus and his students.

The plaster reproduction of the grave stele of Dexileos hung over the mantelpiece of Study Hall (now Livingston) since its construction in 1938 until the 1970s. Originally, this relief and the Amazon Frieze (still in its original location over the Library door in Livingston) belonged to Bryn Mawr School and graced the walls of the Latin Room when Miss Marshall and Miss Offutt were students there. They persuaded their alma mater to sell these two pieces to Garrison Forest School in 1937. Suffering damage and decay from years of storage, the century-old Dexileos sculpture was in almost irreparable condition by the turn of the 21st century. In 2003, Middle School teachers Butch Darrell and Dante Beretta arranged with decorative plaster expert Jon Sampson to restore the relief. It was re-mounted in the new Middle School building in 2007.

D. & J. SMITH EQUESTRIAN CENTER

In 1998, Garrison Forest added a collegiate-quality equestrian center, thus completing a top-level complex for the school's internationally acclaimed riding program. The Smith Center's expansive facilities host numerous GFS and outside horse shows.

MOLLY MUNDY HATHAWAY '61 FINE AND PERFORMING ARTS CENTER

Garrison Forest has an enduring tradition of excellence in the fine and performing arts, but for decades, the classroom and studio spaces to pursue these passions were scattered across campus. In 1996, the school built the Fine and Performing Arts Center to bring the arts together on campus for the first time. It was named in 2005 for Molly Mundy Hathaway '61, who served her alma mater as the consummate fundraiser as director of development and as president of the board from 2000 to 2005. An accomplished artist herself, Molly worked tirelessly to make the school's long-held dream of a central home for the arts a reality.

Students performing in the Hathaway Fine and Performing Arts Center.

The Wendy Byron Smith '55 Art Studio in the former Study Hall, 1950s.

The Molly Mundy Hathaway '61 Fine and Performing Arts Center.

Students enjoying French class outside of Livingston, formerly Study Hall.

The Upper School Library in Study Hall in the 1940s and '50s.

1939

Working on a Tablet PC in the Livingston Library.

LIVINGSTON

From 1937 until the opening of Marshall-Offutt in 1974, Study Hall was an Upper School academic building. Since 1975, the building has served the school's younger students. By the early 1990s, Garrison Forest's Lower School was bursting at the seams. In 1995, Study Hall was expanded and renovated to accommodate the kindergarten through fifth grade program. The building was named Livingston, and a few years later, the Lower School took the same name. (The Preschool program, which is housed in the Moncrieffe Building, was renamed Moncrieffe.) The Livingston building retains its original charm and features, including a shingled exterior and library with its fireplace. In 2000, the school added a unique outdoor feature to Livingston with the creation of the Joan McDonald amphitheatre, which honors the late Mrs. McDonald, a former Middle School Latin teacher, who shared her love of the ancient world with her students and colleagues.

EPILOGUE

"Our motto is embedded not only on our class ring but in our hearts as well: '*Esse Quam Videri*—To Be Rather Than To Seem.' If much 'seems' different, it raises the question about the relevance of that motto. Have we as a school gotten away from 'being' and moved into 'seeming'? My response is a resounding no. The school, our school, is as rooted in authenticity and virtue as the day in 1910 when we adopted that motto. Yes, we do seem different on the external—buildings, uniforms, rules, curriculum, and complexion of our community, and thanks be to God for that difference. What, however, is not different are the unseen things: the commitment to virtue and integrity and intellect and the spirit."

— The Reverend Caroline "Stuart" Rinehart Stewart '66
Garrison Forest School chaplain and trustee

ENDNOTES

1 It is assumed that Miss Livingston's brother Robert Livingston lived with Rev. and Mrs. Hobart Smith around the turn of the 20th century. He died in 1903 at St. Thomas' and is buried in the St. Thomas' cemetery, as are Miss Livingston, her mother, sister, and brother-in-law.

2 Garrison Forest *Alumnae Bulletin*, 1985, *History of Garrison Forest*, by Nancy J. Offutt. "Miss Livingston was promised if she moved her *Lares* and *Penates* to Garrison, would lack neither students nor support. Miss Livingston smiled and said, 'Thank you,' but at the end of the holidays she returned to Kingston. It must have been 'meant' that she should come, however, for in that year [1910] her sister's illness brought Mary Livingston back to Maryland, this time to stay."

3 History does not record Esther Livingston Smith's illness, noting simply in Rev. Smith's obituary in *The Maryland Churchman* (March 1933), that "his wife for many years was a helpless invalid and his love and devotion to her was an inspiration."

4 The date recorded as the first day of Garrison Forest School was September 25, 1910, which was a Sunday. Given Miss Livingston's deep relationship with St. Thomas' and the fact that her brother would have been at the pulpit on Sunday morning—presumably with Miss Livingston, her mother and sister in attendance—it is unlikely that classes were held on a Sunday morning. It is assumed that Nancy Offutt was the source for the date, with several references citing September 25, 1910: GFS *Alumnae Bulletin* 1983-84 (pp. 4-6), school history by Nancy Offutt; GFS *Alumnae Bulletin* 1985-86; undated, transcribed history of school written by Mary McPherson "after N. J. O." (undated interview) with brief history of start of school; *Speaking of Our Past: A Narrative History of Owings Mills, Maryland 1640-1988*, pp. 188-192, Marie Forbes (Heritage Books, 1988); and *The Green Spring Valley: Its History and Heritage*, p. 190, Dawn F. Thomas and Robert Barnes (Maryland Historical Society, 1978). St. Thomas' Church's parish records and Vestry minutes, as well the Maryland Episcopal Diocese Archives, have no record of a convocation or dedication of Miss Livingston's school on September 25, 1910. (In fact, St. Thomas" Vestry minutes from 1909-1913 make no mention of Miss Livingston or any neighborhood school.) The earliest school advertisement was placed in *The Baltimore Sun* on Thursday, September 12, 1911, noting that Miss Livingston could be reached in Ogunquit, Maine until September 20. *Baltimore Sun* ads for other day schools in the region note an early October opening, including an ad for Garrison Forest School in 1912. An ad dated September 19, 1912, states that GFS opened on October 2, 1912. It is assumed that Miss Livingston would have followed, more or less, the schedule of other schools. A 1950s Class News entry with Lois Bryan Wood '20, one of the original students in 1910, talks about when school first opened in October.

5 Upon retiring in 1929, Miss Livingston moved to the Deanery. Her sister Esther Livingston Smith died on December 9, 1929, and Rev. Smith died at the Deanery on January 28, 1933.

6 It is assumed that in 1928-29, Jean Marshall held joint athletic appointments at GFS and Roland Park Country School.

7 According to a 1981 interview between Marie Forbes and Nancy Offutt, Miss Livingston lived in Manor House for the 1929-30 year. The following year, Miss Livingston moved across the street into the Deanery. Later, she moved to the Ten Mile House in Reisterstown, where she entertained her former students and their children during many a Sunday afternoon. Following a devastating fire at the Ten Mile House, Miss Livingston moved to another home in Baltimore before a final move to College Manor in Lutherville, where she died on January 26, 1956.

8 Garrison Forest School Board of Trustee minutes, June 1, 1931. While the Board concurred that students who could not pay full or even partial tuition, but were both strong students and active in school activities, were "…most desirable to have…among the student body,…every possible effort should be made to secure contributions towards scholarships that would at least cover out-of-pocket expenses."

9 "Meet the Press," 1955 *Alumnae Bulletin*, page 8, Nancy Offutt interviewed by Jean Marshall. There are no records to indicate how long the "Special Senior" status lasted. Students were listed as such only in the yearbooks of the 1920s.

10 The phrase *Esse Quam Videri* first appears in "On Friendship" (De amicitia, chapter 98) by Marcus Tullius Cicero, the great Roman statesman. Cicero argues that true friendship is rooted in virtue: "*Virtute enim ipsa non tam multi praediti esse quam Videri volunt.*" ("Many are not so endowed with virtue as they wish to seem"). A few years later, the Roman historian Sallust used the phrase in *Bellum Catilinae* (54.6) to describe the Roman senator Marcus Porcius Cato (95-46 B.C.) or Cato the Younger. Sallust's words, "*Esse quam videri bonus malebat*" ("He preferred to be good rather than to seem so"), describe Cato's unequaled integrity and honesty— the highest of Roman ideals—and his stubborn resistance to Julius Caesar's rise to power. Cato chose suicide rather than acquiesce to Caesar's tyrant hand. During the American Revolution, the Founding Fathers found inspiration for their battle against the British government in the classical works of Greece and Rome. John Adams quoted Cicero and Sallust to rally the Colonists, and General George Washington so admired Cato, the Roman hero about whom Sallust wrote, that he had Joseph Addison's tragedy *Cato* performed for the troops at Valley Forge. The motto enjoyed a resurgence of popularity after John Hay penned a widely published poem entitled *Esse Quam Videri* in honor of William Seward, Abraham Lincoln's Secretary of State. Since it was the Seward family motto, he had it emblazoned on his china.Originally published in 1891 (*Seward at Washington as Senator and Secretary of State: A memoir of his life with selections from his letters* 1861-1872, Frederick W. Seward, New York: Derby and Miller, 1891), the poem was reprinted in an anthology entitled, *Poems with Power to Strengthen the Soul* (compiled and edited by James Mudge. The Abingdon Press: New York, Cincinnati, 1907).

Esse Quam Videri
By John Hay

The knightly legend of thy shield betrays
The moral of thy life; a forecast wise,
And that large honor that deceit defies,
Inspired thy fathers in the elder days,
Who decked thy scutcheon with that sturdy phrase,
"To be rather than seem." As eve's red skies
Surpass the morning's rosy prophecies,

Thy life to that proud boast its answer pays.
Scorning thy faith and purpose to defend
The ever-mutable multitude at last
Will hail the power they did not comprehend,—
Thy fame will broaden through the centuries;
As, storm and billowy tumult overpast,
The moon rules calmly o'er the conquered seas.

REFERENCES

The majority of references for *A Century of Spirit: Garrison Forest School* are from various documents in the school's archives, the sources of which are known and unknown. The author relied heavily upon interviews, school publications, board of trustee minutes and correspondence, etc., and was aided in her research by the following:

Allen, Ethan, Reverend. *The Garrison Church: Sketches of the History of St. Thomas' Parish—Garrison Forest, Baltimore County, Maryland.* New York: James Potts & Company, 1992. Originally published 1898.

Barrymore, Diana and Gerold Frank. *Too Much, Too Soon.* New York: Holt, 1957.

"Dean of P.E. Clergymen Dies of Grippe." *The Maryland Churchman* 30 Jan. 1933: 1.

Forbes, Marie. *Speaking of Our Past: A Narrative History of Owings Mills, Maryland 1640-1988.* Westminster, Maryland: Heritage Books, 1988.

Gillen, William P. "Garrison Forest School to Move," *Baltimore Sun* 11 June 1968: A9.

Hardie, Dee, "School and Family: Happy Combination," *News-Post* 7 Sept. 1962: 6B.

Pell, Eve. *We Used to Own the Bronx: Memoirs of a Former Debutante.* Albany, New York: State University of New York Press, 2009.

Salganik, M. William. "New Chief has Business Acumen," *Baltimore Sun* 24 Sept. 1978: B1 (2 pp.).

Seward, Frederick, W. *Seward at Washington as Senator and Secretary of State: A memoir of his life with selections from his letters 1861-1872.* New York: Derby and Miller, 1891.

Stolley, Richard B. "The Child Seller," *Life* 8 Oct. 1965: 109-116.

Thomas, Dawn F. and Robert Barnes. *The Green Spring Valley: Its History and Heritage.* Baltimore: Maryland Historical Society, 1978.

Whitman, Suzanne Voss White. *The Knoll in the Green Spring Valley, Maryland.* Baltimore: Gateway Press, Inc., 1985.

ACKNOWLEDGMENTS

A great many people assisted in the research and publication of *A Century of Spirit: Garrison Forest School.* Thank you to those who kindly sat through repeated interviews or provided in-depth research: Greta McDonald Anderson '74, Relie Garland Bolton '53, Butch Darrell, genealogist Rod Davis, Bryn Mawr School archivist Elizabeth DiCataldo, French Shriver Foster '42, Doris Hoffman and the other fine volunteers in the Reisterstown Library's Reisterstown Historical Room, Ann Gray, Molly Mundy Hathaway '61, Kitty McLane Hoffman '37, Meg Murray Keech '44, Maryland Episcopal Diocese archivist Mary Klein, Shelia Love '74, Joan Mudge, Barbara Parks at St. Thomas' Church, Lorraine Polvinale, Professors Joshua Kates and Christoph Irmscher in the English Department at Indiana University, Babs Porter, Beth Ruekberg, Stewart Rinehart Stewart '66, Ann Teaff, and Kitty Marshall Washburne '46. A special note of thanks goes to the former and current GFS heads of school who kindly shared their thoughts and papers: Peter O'Neill, Midge Bowman, Anita and the late Tad Montgomery, Linda Hlavacek Silver, and Aggie Underwood.

The majority of images used in the book are from the school's archives, and of both known and unknown origin. The school recognizes the artistry of professional photographers Barton-Gillett Co., Bill Denison, Susie Fitzhugh, Jim Ivey, Steve McDaniel, and Martha Rajkay whose work appears in the book. Image Z6.580 Reisterstown Road is provided courtesy of The Maryland Historical Society, and images P000986.Pikesville and P001906.Meadows, Owings Mills are provided courtesy of The Historical Society of Baltimore County. Garrison Forest kindly thanks *Style* magazine for permission to reprint in part my article, "Mr. Headmaster," *Style*, September/October, 2004. We remain deeply grateful to the following for sharing their photos, letters, badges, uniforms, etc., which are reproduced or referenced herein: Midge Bowman, Judy Booher, Blakely Fetridge Bundy '62, Kati McElderry Curson '90, Cely Elliott, Ann Gray, Pamela Achilles Gould '73, Leigh McDonald Hall '81, Poppy Hall '07, Carrington Dame Hooper '54, Joan Hurley, Jostens, Bee Shriver Kant '54, Bobs Farrel McAleenan '41, Steve McManus, Meadowbrook Aquatic Center, Kingsley Black Moore '54, Peter O'Neill, Nicky Hawes Perry '59, Babs Porter, Carol Harrison Roeder '61, Helen Zinreich Shafer '93, Linda Hlavacek Silver, George Shriver III and the Shriver family, St. Thomas' Church, Alice Painter Thompson '39, the family of the late Carley Havemeyer Wagner '44, Kitty Marshall Washburne '46, and George Wills and the collection of his mother, the late Margaret Marees Wills '24.

Thank you to my Garrison Forest "book group:" Peggy O'Neill for her persistence; Penny Power for her kind resourcefulness; Deanna Gamber Urner '85 for her humor and patience; Paula Einaudi for her love of storytelling and copy-editing; and Denise Harper for her thoroughness. Laura Wexler helped me find my groove, and Sue De Pasquale, Margery Feit, and Dara Zappulla gave their expertise. Designer Wendy Tripp Ruffin '86 added her considerable artistry, good cheer, and flexibility to the herculean task of telling the GFS story. Her eye brought the words to life—thank you. Garrison Forest publications director Ann Doak managed the project with aplomb and the grace of 17 years of friendship—I am in your debt. To GFS archivist Dante Beretta, your motto for the archives—"*Je cherche ce que je ne peux pas trouver*" ("I am looking for what I can't find," from *Le chevalier au Lion* by Chretien de Troyes)—was true more often than we wanted it to be, but I was blessed to have your research prowess, humor, friendship, and coffee during our odyssey.

A very special thanks goes to the wonderful women in the GFS faculty/staff day care. Without your care for my sweet Henry, this book would never have been finished. Thank you, Dee Vanodia, Kay Mistry, Gloria Davies, Sobha Desai, and Sheila Pate. To my family, Jayson, Charlie, and Henry, you have my enduring gratitude. And to Kate Hathaway Bagli '84, the first Garrison girl I met (and still my favorite), thank you for always being and not seeming.

Sarah Achenbach

It was a true pleasure designing this book. I consider it a tribute to the many faculty and staff at Garrison Forest, both past and present, who have influenced and mentored me in so many ways. A heart-felt thank you to all of my teachers while I was a GFS student, including my advisor Francoise von Mayer, headmistress Aggie Underwood, and especially my art teacher B.J. McElderry, who developed my love and passion for art and design and taught me to never give up and to always try to make my artwork better. Thank you to everyone on the book committee for your support, including Peggy O'Neill, Deanna Urner, Dante Beretta, Paula Einaudi, Denise Harper, Penny Power, and particularly Ann Doak for her thoughtful input on this and many other projects over the years, as well as her kind friendship and mentoring. Thank you to the staff at J.W. Boarman, especially Kevin Salter for his dedication to my projects. To the author Sarah Achenbach—we have lived through 100 years together, and I wouldn't change a thing! And finally, a very special thank you to my parents for giving me the opportunity to attend GFS and to my husband Will and daughter Brooke for their constant support each and every day. Brooke, may you learn and grow at GFS as I did, for it is truly the best school in the world!

Wendy Tripp Ruffin '86

So much of the spirit that has infused Garrison Forest School for the past century has come from the faculty, staff, and administrators. In whatever role, these women and men have inspired generations of students through professional and personal examples of integrity, high ideals, and kindness.

In 1992, Garrison Forest began a tradition of presenting a gold pin with the school seal on it to those women and men who reached the 20-year milestone in service to the school. Listed here are the individuals since the school's founding who have spent at least 20 years working for Garrison Forest, encouraging students to be rather than to seem.

Pre-1992		1995	Rufus Davis
	Clinton Arrowood		Ann B. Gray
	Anna Boyd		Edith B. Horney
	Mary Keller Boyd		Brooke P. Pacy
	Elizabeth G. Brown		Stanley P. Zolenas, Jr.
	George Bunting		
	Elizabeth Campbell	1996	Melissa E. Allen
	Calvin Cusey		Charles C. Darrell
	Raymond Duvall		Barbara J. McElderry
	Calvin Cursey		
	Peggy Emmons	1997	Collette M. Wichert
	Coley Gill		
	Roberta Glanville	1998	Karen A. Mallonee
	A. Kathleen Gran		Ann M. Teaff
	Dorothy Hall		
	Mary Victoria Higgs	1999	Ann C. Doak
	Ethel Hoffman		Margery Feit
	Virginia Jones		Brooke T. Gorman
	Mary Moncrieffe Livingston		Nancy B. Kirkland
	Jean Gilmor Marshall		Carlene M. Scott
	Frances Matthai		Michele Y. Shepherd
	Nancy Jenkins Offutt		Francoise von Mayer
	Rhoda Penrose		
	Mary Purdy	2000	Martha S. Hankins
	Anna Sterrett		
	Noreen Taylor	2001	Janet C. Partel
	Miriam Vanderveer		Julia Wright
	Mary Adelaide Wagner		
	Lucette Wallace	2002	Clover P. Roulette
	Alfred West		Penny F. Miller
	Louise West		Micul Ann Morse
	Elizabeth White		Arden F. Scott
	Margretta Whiting		
	Suzanne White Whitman	2003	Judith M. Booher
	Palmer F.C. Williams		Valerie Marsh
	Al Woodhouse		Penelope R. Power
1992	Cielito O. Elliott	2004	Audrey M. Crooks
	Donald S. Elliott, Jr.		Francis J. Miller, Jr.
	Irene Jackson *		Sue Z. Sternheimer
	Micheline Johnson		
	Dorothy Kelley	2005	Tina B. Moran
	Winifred P. McDowell		Deborah F. Oleisky
	Irvin D. McGregor		
	Joan W. Mudge	2006	Virginia S. Berrier
	Dorothy M. Peltzer		Kimberley J. Marlor
	Lorraine K. Polvinale		Louise W. Smith
	Barbara H. Porter *		
	Theresa I. Skinner	2007	Dante G. Beretta, Jr.
	Joan F. Smith		Elizabeth G. Ruekberg
	Elizabeth R. Simpson *		
		2008	Janet R. Havlik
			Louise S. Moran
1994	Genevieve R. Murray		
	Carol B. Peabody	2009	A. Randol Benedict '76
	Jane M. Saral		William S. Hodgetts
	Susan F. Weiss		Sanford M. Racher

*Retired before the award was established. The names on the pre-1992 list are as accurate as early school records allow.